History of Islam in Europe

Compiled by
Pandora Ruff

Scribbles

Year of Publication 2018

ISBN : 9789352979219

Book Published by

Scribbles

(An Imprint of Alpha Editions)

email - alphaedis@gmail.com

Produced by: PediaPress GmbH
Limburg an der Lahn
Germany
http://pediapress.com/

The content within this book was generated collaboratively by volunteers. Please be advised that nothing found here has necessarily been reviewed by people with the expertise required to provide you with complete, accurate or reliable information. Some information in this book may be misleading or simply wrong. Alpha Editions and PediaPress does not guarantee the validity of the information found here. If you need specific advice (for example, medical, legal, financial, or risk management) please seek a professional who is licensed or knowledgeable in that area.

Sources, licenses and contributors of the articles and images are listed in the section entitled "References". Parts of the books may be licensed under the GNU Free Documentation License. A copy of this license is included in the section entitled "GNU Free Documentation License"

The views and characters expressed in the book are those of the contributors and his/her imagination and do not represent the views of the Publisher.

Contents

Articles   **1**

Introduction   **1**
    Islam in Europe 1

History   **21**
    Moors 21
    Al-Andalus 41
    Emirate of Sicily 65
    Islamic world contributions to Medieval Europe 76
    Reception of Islam in Early Modern Europe 99

Appendix   **111**
    References 111
    Article Sources and Contributors 120
    Image Sources, Licenses and Contributors 121

Article Licenses   **125**

Index   **127**

Introduction

Islam in Europe

Islam is the second largest religious belief in Europe after Christianity.Wikipedia:Citation needed Although the majority of Muslim communities in Europe are of recent migrations, there are pre-Modern ones in the Balkans.

Islam entered southern Europe through the invading "Moors" of North Africa in the 8th–10th centuries; Muslim political entities existed firmly in what is today Spain, Portugal, South Italy and Malta for several centuries. The Muslim community in these territories was converted or expelled by the end of the 15th century (see *Reconquista*). Islam expanded into the Caucasus through the Muslim conquest of Persia in the 7th century. The Ottoman Empire expanded into southeastern Europe, invading and conquering huge portions of the Byzantine Empire in the 14th and 15th centuries. Over the centuries, the Ottoman Empire also gradually lost almost all of its European territories, until the empire collapsed in 1922. The countries of the Balkans continue to have large populations of native Muslims, though the majority are unobservant or secular.

The term "Muslim Europe" is used for the Muslim-majority countries of Albania, Kosovo and Bosnia and Herzegovina. Transcontinental countries, such as Turkey, Azerbaijan and Kazakhstan have large Muslim populations, as does Russia in the North Caucasus.

In the late 20th and early 21st centuries substantial numbers of Muslims immigrated to Western Europe. By 2010 an estimated 44 million Muslims were living in Europe (6%), including an estimated 19 million in the EU (3.8%). They are projected to comprise 8% by 2030.Wikipedia:Citation needed They are often the subject of intense discussion and political campaigns. These have been periodically revived by events such as terrorist attacks by Islamists, the cartoons affair in Denmark, debates over Islamic dress, and ongoing support

1

Figure 1:
Islam in Europe
by percentage of country population

for populist right-wing parties that view Muslims as a threat to European values, culture and ways of life. Such events have also fueled growing debate regarding the topic of Islamophobia, attitudes toward Muslims and the populist right

History

The Muslim population in Europe is extremely diverse with varied histories and origins. Today, the Muslim-majority regions of Europe are Bosnia and Herzegovina, Albania, Kosovo, parts of Macedonia and Montenegro, as well as some Russian regions in Northern Caucasus and the Volga region. The communities consist predominantly of indigenous Europeans of the Muslim faith whose religious tradition dates back several hundred years. The transcontinental countries of Turkey, Azerbaijan and Kazakhstan also are Muslim majority.

Figure 2: *The Moors request permission from James I of Aragon, Spain, 13th century*

Moors, Al-Andalus and Sicily

Muslim forays into Europe began shortly after the religion's inception, with a short-lived invasion of Byzantine Sicily by a small Arab and Berber force that landed in 652. Islam gained its first genuine foothold in continental Europe from 711 onward, with the Umayyad conquest of Hispania. The Arabs renamed the land Al-Andalus, which expanded to include the larger parts of what is now Portugal and Spain except for the northern highlands. It is estimated that Al-Andalus had a Muslim majority by the 10th century after most of the local population willingly converted to Islam.[1] This coincided with the *La Convivencia* period of the Iberian Peninsula as well as the Golden age of Jewish culture in Spain. The Christian counter-offensive known as the *Reconquista* began in the early 8th century, when Muslim forces managed to temporarily push into southern France. Slowly, the Christian forces began a re-conquest of the fractured Taifa kingdoms of Al-Andalus. There was still a Muslim presence north of Spain, especially in Fraxinet all the way into Switzerland until the 10th century.[2] Muslim forces under the Aghlabids conquered Sicily after a series of expeditions spanning 827–902, and had notably raided Rome in 846. The Emirate of Sicily was established in 965. Arabs held onto southern Italy until their expulsion by the Normans in 1072. By 1236, practically all that remained of Muslim Spain was the southern province of Granada.

Figure 3: *"Araz" coat of arms of Polish Tatar nobility. Tatar coats of arms often included motifs related to Islam.*

The Arabs imposed Sharia, thus, the Latin- and Greek-speaking Christian communities, as well as a community of Jews, had limited freedom of religion under the Muslims as *dhimmi* (non-Muslims). They were required to pay *jizya* (poll tax), *kharaj* (land tax), but exempt from the Muslim tax of *zakaat*. These taxes marked their status as subject to Muslim rule, albeit in exchange for protection against foreign and internal aggression.

Cultural impact and interaction

Arabic-speaking Christian scholars saved influential pre-Christian texts and introduced aspects of medieval Islamic culture[3] (including the arts,[4,5,6] economics,[7] science and technology).[8,9] (See Latin translations of the 12th century and Islamic contributions to Medieval Europe for more information).

Muslim rule endured in the Emirate of Granada, from 1238 as a vassal state of the Christian Kingdom of Castile, until the completion of La Reconquista in 1492.[10] The Moriscos (Moorish in Spanish) were finally expelled from Spain between 1609 (Castile) and 1614 (rest of Spain), by Philip III during the Spanish Inquisition.

Throughout the 16th to 19th centuries, the Barbary States sent pirates to raid nearby parts of Europe in order to capture Christian slaves to sell at slave

Figure 4: *The Great Mosque of Paris, built after World War I.*

markets in the Arab World throughout the Renaissance period. According to Robert Davis, from the 16th to 19th centuries, pirates captured 1 million to 1.25 million Europeans as slaves. These slaves were captured mainly from the crews of captured vessels[11] and from coastal villages in Spain and Portugal, and from farther places like Italy, France or England, the Netherlands, Ireland, the Azores Islands, and even Iceland.

For a long time, until the early 18th century, the Crimean Khanate maintained a massive slave trade with the Ottoman Empire and the Middle East.[12] The Crimean Tatars frequently mounted raids into the Danubian principalities, Poland-Lithuania, and Russia to enslave people whom they could capture.[13]

Hungary

The Böszörmény Muslims formed an early community of Muslims in Hungary. Their biggest settlement was near the town of present-day Orosháza in the central part of the Hungarian Kingdom. At that time this settlement entirely populated by Muslims was probably one of the biggest settlements of the Kingdom. This and several other Muslim settlements were all destroyed and their inhabitants massacred during the 1241 Mongol invasion of Hungary.

Figure 5: *Log pod Mangartom Mosque was the only mosque ever built in Slovenia, in the town of Log pod Mangartom, during World War I.*

Russia and Ukraine

In the mid-7th century AD, following the Muslim conquest of Persia, it spread into areas that would later become part of Russia. There are accounts of the trade connections between the Muslims and the Rus, apparently people from Baltic region who made their way towards the Black Sea through Central Russia. On his way to Volga Bulgaria, Ibn Fadlan brought detailed reports of the Rus, claiming that some had converted to Islam. "They are very fond of pork and many of them who have assumed the path of Islam miss it very much." The Rus also relished their *nabidh*, a fermented drink Ibn Fadlan often mentioned as part of their daily fare.[14]

The Mongols began their conquest of Rus', Volga Bulgaria, and the Cuman-Kipchak Confederation (present day Russia and Ukraine) in the 13th century. After the Mongol empire split, the eastern European section became known as the Golden Horde. Despite the fact that they were not Muslim at the time, the western Mongols adopted Islam as their religion in the early 14th century under Berke Khan, and later Uzbeg Khan who established it as the official religion of the state. Much of the mostly Turkic-speaking population of the Horde, as well as the small Mongol aristocracy, were Islamized (if they were not already Muslim, such as the Volga Bulgars) and became known to Russians and Europeans as the Tatars. More than half of the European portion of what is now Russia and Ukraine, were under the suzerainty of Muslim Tatars

Figure 6: *The Ottoman campaign for territorial expansion in Europe in 1566, Crimean Tatars as vanguard.*

and Turks from the 13th to 15th centuries. The Crimean Khanate became a vassal state of the Ottoman Empire in 1475 and subjugated what remained of the Great Horde by 1502. The Khanate of Kazan was conquered by Ivan the Terrible in 1552.

Belarus and Poland-Lithuania

Lipka Tatar Muslims of Belarus and Poland-Lithuania. The material of their Mosques is wood.

Ottoman Empire and the Balkans

The Ottoman Empire began its expansion into Europe by taking the European portions of the Byzantine Empire in the 14th and 15th centuries up until the 1453 capture of Constantinople, establishing Islam as the state religion in the region. The Ottoman Empire continued to stretch northwards, taking Hungary in the 16th century, and reaching as far north as the Podolia in the mid-17th century (Peace of Buczacz), by which time most of the Balkans was under Ottoman control. Ottoman expansion in Europe ended with their defeat in the Great Turkish War. In the Treaty of Karlowitz (1699), the Ottoman Empire lost most of its conquests in Central Europe. The Crimean Khanate was later

Figure 7: *The Ottoman Sultan Suleiman the Magnificent, awaits the arrival of his Greek Muslim Grand Vizier Pargalı Ibrahim Pasha at Buda, in the year 1529.*

Figure 8: *Medieval Bulgaria particularly the city of Sofia, was the administrative centre of almost all Ottoman possessions in the Balkans also known as Rumelia.*

Figure 9: *Painting of the bazaar at Athens, Ottoman Greece, early 19th century*

annexed by Russia in 1783. Over the centuries, the Ottoman Empire gradually lost almost all of its European territories, until its collapse in 1922, when the former empire was transformed into the nation of Turkey.Wikipedia:Citation needed

Between 1354 (when the Ottomans crossed into Europe at Gallipoli) and 1526, the Empire had conquered the territory of present-day Greece, Bulgaria, Romania, Albania, Serbia, Macedonia, Montenegro, Bosnia, and Hungary. The Empire laid siege to Vienna in 1683. The intervention of the Polish King broke the siege, and from then afterwards the Ottomans battled the Habsburg Emperors until 1699, when the Treaty of Karlowitz forced them to surrender Hungary and portions of present-day Croatia, Slovenia, and Serbia. From 1699 to 1913, wars and insurrections pushed the Ottoman Empire further back until it reached the current European border of present-day Turkey.Wikipedia:Citation needed

For most of this period, the Ottoman retreats were accompanied by Muslim refugees from these provinces (in almost all cases converts from the previous subject populations), leaving few Muslim inhabitants in Hungary, Croatia, and the Transylvania region of present-day Romania. Bulgaria remained under Ottoman rule until around 1878, and currently its population includes about 131,000 Muslims (2001 Census) (see Pomaks).

Bosnia was conquered by the Ottomans in 1463, and a large portion of the population converted to Islam in the first 200 years of Ottoman domination.

Figure 10: *Registration of Christian boys for the tribute in blood. Ottoman miniature painting, 1558.*

By the time Austria-Hungary occupied Bosnia in 1878, the Habsburgs had shed the desire to re-Christianize new provinces. As a result, a sizable Muslim population in Bosnia survived into the 20th century. Albania and the Kosovo area remained under Ottoman rule until 1913. Prior to the Ottoman conquest, the northern Albanians were Roman Catholic and the southern Albanians were Christian Orthodox, but by 1913 the majority were Muslim.Wikipedia:Citation needed

Conversion to Islam

Apart from the effect of a lengthy period under Ottoman domination, many of the subject population were converted to Islam as a result of a deliberate move by the Ottomans as part of a policy of ensuring the loyalty of the population against a potential Venetian invasion. However, Islam was spread by force in the areas under the control of the Ottoman Sultan through devşirme and jizya.[15,16] Rather Arnold explains Islam's spread by quoting 17th-century pro-MuslimWikipedia:Citation needed author Johannes Scheffler who stated:

" Meanwhile he (i.e. the Turk) wins (converts) by craft more than by force, and snatches away Christ by fraud out of the hearts of men. For the Turk, it is true, at the present time compels no country by violence to apostatise; but he uses other means whereby imperceptibly he roots out Christianity... What then has become of the Christians? They are not expelled from the country, neither are they forced to embrace the Turkish faith: then they must of themselves have been converted into Turks.[17] "

Cultural influences

Islam piqued interest among European scholars, setting off the movement of Orientalism. The founder of modern Islamic studies in Europe was Ignác Goldziher, who began studying Islam in the late 19th century. For instance, Sir Richard Francis Burton, 19th-century English explorer, scholar, and orientalist, and translator of *The Book of One Thousand and One Nights*, disguised himself as a Pashtun and visited both Medina and Mecca during the Hajj, as described in his book *A Personal Narrative of a Pilgrimage to Al-Medinah and Meccah*.

Islamic architecture influenced European architecture in various ways (for example, the Türkischer Tempel synagogue in Vienna). During the 12th-century Renaissance in Europe, Latin translations of Arabic texts were introduced. The Koran was also translated (for example, Lex Mahumet pseudoprophete).

Twentieth century

Muslim emigration to metropolitan France surged during the Algerian War of Independence.Wikipedia:Citation needed In 1961, the West German Government invited first Gastarbeiters and similar contracts were offered by Switzerland; some of these migrant workers came from majority-Muslim countries such as Turkey.Wikipedia:Citation needed Migrants came to Britain from its majority-Muslim former colonies Pakistan and Bangladesh.Wikipedia:Citation needed

Current demographics

The exact number of Muslims in Europe is unknown. According to estimates by the Pew Forum, the total number of Muslims in Europe (excluding Turkey) in 2010 was about 44 million (6% of the total population), including 19 million (3.8% of the population) in the European Union.[18]

Approximately 9 million Turks are living in Europe, excluding the Turkish population of Turkey, which makes up the largest Muslim immigrant community in Europe. Estimates of the percentage of Muslims in Russia (the biggest group of Muslims in Europe) vary from 5[19] to 11.7%,[18] depending on sources.

Figure 11: *The King's Mosque (Pristina) of Sultan Mehmet Fatih in Pristina, Kosovo*

Figure 12: *Muslim-majority areas in Europe*

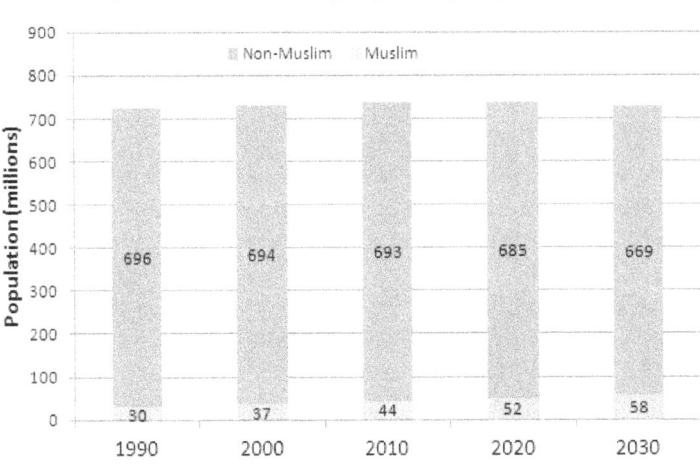

Figure 13: *According to the Pew Research Center, Europe's population was 6% Muslim in 2010, and is projected to be 8% Muslim by 2030.*[18] *(The data does not reckon illegal immigration from the Middle East and Africa since the migration crisis.)*

It also depends on if only observant Muslims or all people of Muslim descent are counted.

58.8% of Albania adheres to Islam, making it the largest religion in the country. The majority of Albanian Muslims are Secular Sunni with a significant Bektashi Shia minority.[20] The percentage is 93.5% in Kosovo, 39.3% in Macedonia[21,22] (according to the 2002 Census, 46.5% of the children aged 0–4 were Muslim in Macedonia)[23] and 50.7% in Bosnia and Herzegovina.[24] In transcontinental countries such as Turkey 99%, and 93% in Azerbaijan of the population is Muslim respectively. According to the 2011 census, 20% of the total population in Montenegro are Muslims.[25] In Russia, Moscow is home to an estimated 1.5 million Muslims.[26,27,28]

Projections

A Pew Research Center study, published in January 2011, forecast an increase of Muslims in European population from 6% in 2010 to 8% in 2030.[18] The study also predicted that Muslim fertility rate in Europe would drop from 2.2 in 2010 to 2.0 in 2030. On the other hand, the non-Muslim fertility rate in Europe would increase from 1.5 in 2010 to 1.6 in 2030.[18] Another Pew study published in 2017 projected that in 2050 Muslims will make 7.4% (if all migration into Europe were to immediately and permanently stop - a "zero migration" scenario) up to 14% (under a "high" migration scenario) of Europe's population. Data from the 2000s for the rates of growth of Islam in Europe showed that the growing number of Muslims was due primarily to immigration and higher birth rates.

In 2017, Pew projected that the Muslim population of Europe would reach a level between 7% and 14% by 2050. The projections depend on the level of migration. With no net migration, the projected level was 7%; with high migration, it was 14%. The projections varied greatly by country. Under the high migration scenario, the highest projected level of any historically non-Muslim country was 30% in Sweden. By contrast, Poland was projected to remain below 1%.

In 2006, the conservative Christian historian Philip Jenkins, in an article for the Foreign Policy Research Institute thinktank, wrote that by 2100, a Muslim population of about 25% of Europe's population was "probable"; Jenkins stated this figure did not take account growing birthrates amongst Europe's immigrant Christians, but did not give details of his methodology.[29] in 2010, Eric Kaufmann, professor of politics at Birkbeck, University of London said that "In our projections for Western Europe by 2050 we are looking at a range of 10-15 per cent Muslim population for most of the high immigration countries – Germany, France, the UK"; he argued that Islam was expanding, not because of conversion to Islam, but primarily due to the religion's "pro-natal" orientation, where Muslims tend to have more children.Wikipedia:Citation needed Other analysts are skeptical about the accuracy of the claimed Muslim population growth, stating that because many European countries do not ask a person's religion on official forms or in censuses, it has been difficult to obtain accurate estimates, and arguing that there has been a decrease in Muslim fertility rates in Morocco, the Netherlands and Turkey.[30]

A 2007 Center for Strategic and International Studies (CSIS) report argued that some Muslim population projections may be overestimated, as they assume that all descendants of Muslims will become Muslims even in cases of mixed parenthood.[31] Equally, Darren E. Sherkat questioned in *Foreign Affairs* whether some of the Muslim growth projections are accurate as they do not take into account the increasing number of non-religious Muslims. Quantitative research is lacking, but he believes the European trend mirrors the American: data from the General Social Survey in the United States show that 32 percent of those raised Muslim no longer embrace Islam in adulthood, and 18 percent hold no religious identification.

Table, Islam by country

Islam in Europe

Country	Muslims (official)	Muslims (estimation)	% of total population	% of World Muslim population	Community origin (predominant)
Albania	1,646,128	2,601,000 (Pew 2011)	58.79 (official);[32] 82.1 (Pew 2011)	0.1	Indigenous (Albanians)
Andorra	N/A	< 1,000 (Pew 2011)	< 0.1	< 0.1	Immigrant
Austria	N/A	700,000 (2017 study)	8	< 0.1	Immigrant
Belarus	N/A	19,000 (Pew 2011)	0.2	< 0.1	Immigrant
Belgium	N/A	781,887 (2015 est.)	5.9–7	< 0.1	Immigrant
Bosnia-Herzegovina	1,790,454 (2016 census)	1,564,000 (Pew 2011)	50.7 (official); 41.6 (Pew 2011)	0.1	Indigenous (Bosniaks)
Bulgaria	577,000 (2011 census)	1,002,000 (Pew 2011)	7.8 (official); 13.4 (Pew 2011)	< 0.1	Indigenous (Pomaks, Turks)
Croatia	N/A	56,000 (Pew 2011)	1.3 (Pew 2011)	< 0.1	Immigrant
Cyprus	N/A	200,000 (Pew 2011)	22.7 (Pew 2011)	< 0.1	Indigenous (Turks)
Czech Republic	N/A	4,000 (Pew 2011)	< 0.1	< 0.1	Immigrant
Denmark	N/A	226,000 (Pew 2011)	4.1 (Pew 2011)	< 0.1	Immigrant
Estonia	1,508	2,000	0.1 (Pew 2011)	< 0.1	Immigrant
Faroe Islands	N/A	< 1,000 (Pew 2011)	< 0.1	< 0.1	Immigrant
Finland	N/A	150,000 (Pew 2016)	2.7 (Pew 2016)	<0.1	Immigrant
France	N/A	4,704,000 (Pew 2011)	7.5 (Pew 2011)	0.3	Immigrant
Germany	N/A	4,119,000 (Pew 2011); 4,700,000 (CIA)	5 (Pew 2011)	0.2	Immigrant
Greece	N/A	527,000 (Pew 2011)	4.7 (Pew 2011)	<0.1	Indigenous (minority)
Hungary	5,579	25,000 (Pew 2011)	0.3 (Pew 2011)	<0.1	Immigrant
Iceland	770	< 1,000 (Pew 2011)	0.2	<0.1	Immigrant
Ireland	70,158 (2016 census)	43,000 (Pew 2011)	1.3	<0.1	Immigrant
Italy	N/A	1,583,000 (Pew 2011)	2.3;[33] 2.6 (Pew 2011)	0.1	Immigrant

Country					
Kosovo	N/A	1,584,000 (CIA); 2,104,000 (Pew 2011)	95.6	0.1	Indigenous (Albanians)
Latvia	N/A	2,000 (Pew 2011)	0.1	<0.1	Immigrant
Liechtenstein	N/A	2,000 (Pew 2011)	4.8 (Pew 2011)	<0.1	Immigrant
Lithuania	N/A	3,000 (Pew 2011)	0.1 (Pew 2011)	<0.1	Immigrant
Luxembourg	N/A	11,000 (Pew 2011)	2.3 (Pew 2011)	<0.1	Immigrant
Macedonia	N/A	713,000 (Pew 2011)	34.9 (Pew 2011)	<0.1	Indigenous (Albanians, Turks, Romani)
Malta	N/A	1,000 (Pew 2011)	0.3 (Pew 2011)	<0.1	Immigrant
Moldova	N/A	15,000 (Pew 2011)	0.4 (Pew 2011)	< 0.1	Immigrant
Monaco	N/A	< 1,000 (Pew 2011)	0.5 (Pew 2011)	< 0.1	Immigrant
Montenegro	118,477 (2011)	116,000 (Pew 2011)	19.11	< 0.1	Indigenous (Bosniaks, Albanians, "Muslims")
Netherlands	N/A	914,000 (Pew 2011)	5–6	0.1	Immigrant
Norway	N/A	106,700–194,000 (Brunborg & Østby 2011);	2–4	< 0.1	Immigrant
Poland	N/A	20,000 (Pew 2011)	0.1 (Pew 2011)	< 0.1	Immigrant
Portugal	N/A	65,000 (Pew 2011)	0.6 (Pew 2011)	< 0.1	Immigrant
Romania	N/A	73,000 (Pew 2011)	0.3 (Pew 2011)	< 0.1	Indigenous (Turks and Tatars)
Russia	N/A	16,379,000 (Pew 2011)	11.7 (Pew 2011); 15 (CIA))	1.0	Indigenous
San Marino	N/A	< 1,000 (Pew 2011)	< 0.1	< 0.1	Immigrant
Serbia	228,828 (2011)	280,000 (Pew 2011)	3.1 (CIA); 3.7 (Pew 2011)	< 0.1	Indigenous (Bosniaks, "Muslims", Albanians)
Slovakia	10,866	4,000 (Pew 2011)	0.1 (Pew 2011)	< 0.1	Immigrant

Slovenia	73,568	49,000 (Pew 2011)	2.4 (Pew 2011)	< 0.1	Immigrant
Spain	1,887,906	1,021,000 (Pew 2011)	4.1	0.1	Immigrant
Sweden	N/A	450–500,000 (2009 DRL); 451,000 (Pew 2011)	5	< 0.1	Immigrant
Switzerland	N/A	433,000	5.7 (Pew 2011)	< 0.1	Immigrant
Ukraine	N/A	393,000 (Pew 2011)	0.9 (Pew 2011)	< 0.1	Immigrant
United Kingdom	3,106,368	2,869,000 (Pew 2011)	4.6 (Pew 2011)	0.2	Immigrant

Society

Fundamenalism

A 2013 study by Wissenschaftszentrum Berlin für Sozialforschung (WZB) found that Islamic fundamentalism was widespread among Muslims in Europe. The study conducted a poll among Turkish immgrants to six European countries: Germany, France, the Netherlands, Belgium, Austria and Sweden. In the first four countries also Moroccan immigrants were interviewed. Fundametalism was defined as: the belief that believers should return to the eternal and unchangeable rules laid down in the past; that these rules allow only one interpretation and are binding for all believers; and that religious rules have priority over secular laws. Two thirds of Muslims the majority responded that religious rules are more important than civil laws and three quarters rejecting religious pluralism within Islam. Of the respondents, 44% agreed to all three statements. Almost 60% responded that Muslims should return to the roots of Islam, 75% thought there was only one possible interpretation of the Quran.

The conclusion was that religious fundamentalism is much more prevalent among European Muslims than among Christian natives.

Figure 14: *Mosque of Rome, in Rome, the largest in the EU*

Figure 15: *The East London Mosque was one of the first in Britain to be allowed to use loudspeakers to broadcast the adhan.*

Attitudes towards Muslims

The European Monitoring Centre on Racism and Xenophobia reports that the Muslim population tends to suffer Islamophobia all over Europe, although the perceptions and views of Muslims may vary.[35]

A 2015 poll by the Polish Centre for Public Opinion Research found that 44% of Poles have a negative attitude towards Muslims, with only 23% having a positive attitude towards them. Furthermore, a majority agreed with statements like "Muslims are intolerant of customs and values other than their own." (64% agreed, 12% disagreed), "Muslims living in Western European countries generally do not acquire customs and values that are characteristic for the majority of the population of that country." (63% agreed, 14% disagreed), "Islam encourages violence more than other religions." (51% agreed, 24% disagreed)

Further reading

- Ghodsee, Kristen (2009). *Muslim Lives in Eastern Europe: Gender, Ethnicity and the Transformation of Islam in Postsocialist Bulgaria*[36]. Princeton: Princeton University Press. ISBN 978-0-691-13955-5.
- König, Daniel G., Arabic-Islamic Views of the Latin West. Tracing the Emergence of Medieval Europe, Oxford, OUP, 2015.
- Hamza, Gabor, Zur Rolle des Islam in der Geschichte des ungarischen Rechts. Revista Europea de Historia de las Ideas Políticas y de las Instituciones Públicas (REHIPIP) Número 3 - Junio 2012 1-11.pp. http://www.eumed.net/rev/rehipip/03/gh.pdf

- Uwe Halbach. "Islam in the North Caucasus"[37]. pp. 93–110.

External links

- "Muslim Population by Country"[38]. *The Future of the Global Muslim Population*. Pew Research Center. 27 January 2011. Archived from the original[39] on 9 February 2011. Retrieved 22 December 2011.
- For Muslim Minorities, it is Possible to Endorse Political Liberalism, But This is not Enough[40]
- BBC News: Muslims in Europe[41]
- Khabrein.info: Barroso: Islam is part of Europe[42]
- Euro-Islam Website Coordinator Jocelyne Cesari, Harvard University and CNRS-GSRL, Paris[43]
- [44][45]
- Asabiyya: Re-Interpreting Value Change in Globalized Societies[46]
- Why Europe has to offer a better deal towards its Muslim communities. A quantitative analysis of open international data[47]
- Köchler, Hans, *Muslim-Christian Ties in Europe: Past, Present and Future*[48], 1996
- "Islam in Europe: A Resource Guide"[49]. USA: New York Public Library. 2011.

History

Moors

The term "**Moors**" refers primarily to the Muslim inhabitants of the Maghreb, the Iberian Peninsula, Sicily, Sardinia, Corsica, and Malta during the Middle Ages. The Moors initially were the indigenous Maghrebine Berbers. The name was later also applied to Arabs.[50,51]

Moors are not a distinct or self-defined people,[52] and the 1911 Encyclopædia Britannica observed that "The term 'Moors' has no real ethnological value." Europeans of the Middle Ages and the early modern period variously applied the name to Arabs, North African Berbers, and Muslim Europeans.

The term has also been used in Europe in a broader, somewhat derogatory sense to refer to Muslims in general,[53] especially those of Arab or Berber descent, whether living in Spain or North Africa. During the colonial era, the Portuguese introduced the names "Ceylon Moors" and "Indian Moors" in Sri Lanka, and the Bengali Muslims were also called Moors.[54] In the Philippines, the longstanding Muslim community, which predates the arrival of the Spanish, now self-identifies as the "Moro people", an exonym introduced by Spanish colonizers due to their Muslim faith.

In 711, troops mostly formed by Moors from northern Africa led the Umayyad conquest of Hispania. The Iberian peninsula then came to be known in Classical Arabic as al-Andalus, which at its peak included most of Septimania and modern-day Spain and Portugal.

In 827, the Moors occupied Mazara on Sicily, developing it as a port. They eventually consolidated the rest of the island and some of southern Italy. Differences in religion and culture led to a centuries-long conflict with the Christian kingdoms of Europe, which tried to reclaim control of Muslim areas; this conflict was referred to as the Reconquista. In 1224 the Muslims were expelled from Sicily to the settlement of Lucera, which was destroyed by European Christians in 1300.

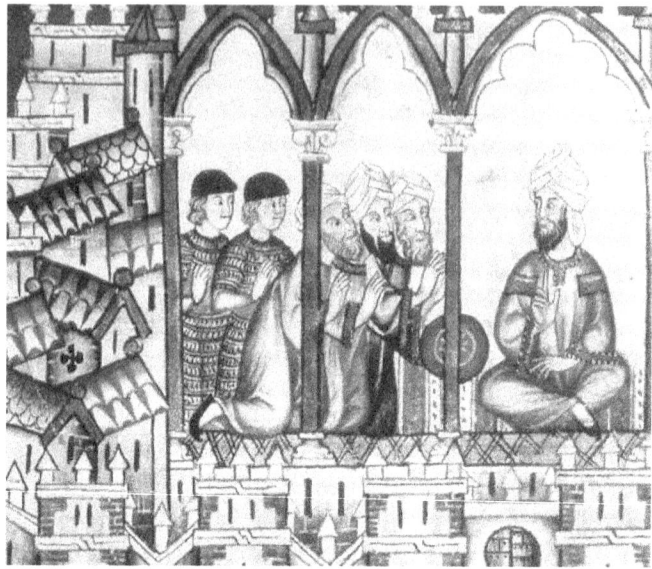

Figure 16: *Castillian ambassadors attempting to convince Moorish Almohad king Abu Hafs Umar al-Murtada to join their alliance (contemporary depiction from the Cantigas de Santa María)*

The fall of Granada in 1492 marked the end of Muslim rule in Iberia, although a Muslim minority persisted until their expulsion in 1609.

Name

Etymology

During the classical period, the Romans interacted with, and later conquered, parts of Mauretania, a state that covered modern northern Morocco, western Algeria, and the Spanish cities Ceuta and Melilla. The Berber tribes of the region were noted in the Classics as *Mauri*, which was subsequently rendered as "Moors" in English and in related variations in other European languages. *Mauri* (Μαῦροι) is recorded as the native name by Strabo in the early 1st century. This appellation was also adopted into Latin, whereas the Greek name for the tribe was *Maurusii* (Ancient Greek: Μαυρούσιοι).[55] The Moors were also mentioned by Tacitus as having revolted against the Roman Empire in 24 AD.[56]

During the Latin Middle Ages, *Mauri* was used to refer to Berbers and Arabs in the coastal regions of Northwest Africa. The 16th century scholar Leo

Africanus (c. 1494–1554) identified the Moors (*Mauri*) as the native Berber inhabitants of the former Roman Africa Province (Roman Africans). He described Moors as one of five main population groups on the continent alongside Egyptians, Abyssinians (Abassins), Arabians and Cafri (Cafates).

The term was commonly used as a racial designation for dark-skinned or black peoples, as with its use in English, seen as early as the fourteenth century.

Modern meanings

In medieval Romance languages, variations of the Latin word for the Moors (for instance, Italian and Spanish: *moro*, French: *maure*, Portuguese: *mouro*, Romanian: *maur*) developed different applications and connotations. The term initially denoted a specific Berber people in western Libya, but the name acquired more general meaning during the medieval period, associated with "Muslim", similar to associations with "Saracens". During the context of the Crusades and the Reconquista, the term Moors included the derogatory suggestion of "infidels".

Apart from these historic associations and context, *Moor* and *Moorish* designate a specific ethnic group speaking Hassaniya Arabic. They inhabit Mauritania and parts of Algeria, Western Sahara, Tunisia, Morocco, Niger, and Mali. In Niger and Mali, these peoples are also known as the Azawagh Arabs, after the Azawagh region of the Sahara.[57]

The authoritative dictionary of the Spanish language does not list any derogatory meaning for the word *moro*, a term generally referring to people of Maghrebian origin in particular or Muslims in general.[58] Some authors have pointed out that in modern colloquial Spanish use of the term *moro* is derogatory for Moroccans in particular and Muslims in general.

In modern, colloquial Portuguese, the term *Mouro* was primarily used as a designation for North Africans and secondarily as a derogatory and ironic term by northern Portuguese to refer to the inhabitants of the southern parts of the country (Lisbon, Alentejo, and Algarve). However, this designation has gained more acceptance in the south.

In the Philippines, a former Spanish colony, many modern Filipinos call the large, local Muslim minority concentrated in Mindanao and other southern islands *Moros*. The word is a catch-all term, as *Moro* may come from several distinct ethno-linguistic groups such as the Maranao people. The term was introduced by Spanish colonisers, and has since been appropriated by Filipino Muslims as an endonym, with many self-identifying as members of the *Bangsamoro* "Moro Nation".

Moreno can mean *dark-skinned* in Spain, Portugal, Brazil, and the Philippines. Also in Spanish, *morapio* is a humorous name for "wine", especially that which has not been "baptized" or mixed with water, i.e., pure unadulterated wine. Among Spanish speakers, *moro* came to have a broader meaning, applied to both Filipino Moros from Mindanao, and the moriscos of Granada. *Moro* refers to all things dark, as in "Moor", *moreno*, etc. It was also used as a nickname; for instance, the Milanese Duke Ludovico Sforza was called *Il Moro* because of his dark complexion.[59]

In Portugal, *mouro* (feminine, *moura*) may refer to supernatural beings known as enchanted *moura*, where "moor" implies 'alien' and 'non-Christian'. These beings were siren-like fairies with golden or reddish hair and a fair face. They were believed to have magical properties.[60] From this root, the name moor is applied to unbaptized children, meaning not Christian.[61,62] In Basque, *mairu* means moor and also refers to a mythical people.[63]

Within the context of Portuguese colonization, in Sri Lanka (Portuguese Ceylon), Muslims of Arab origin are called *Ceylon Moors*, not to be confused with "Indian Moors" of Sri Lanka (see Sri Lankan Moors). Sri Lankan Moors (a combination of "Ceylon Moors" and "Indian Moors") make up 12% of the population. The Ceylon Moors (unlike the Indian Moors) are descendants of Arab traders who settled there in the mid-6th century. When the Portuguese arrived in the early 16th century, they labelled all the Muslims in the island as Moors as they saw some of them resembling the Moors in North Africa. The Sri Lankan government continues to identify the Muslims in Sri Lanka as "Sri Lankan Moors", sub-categorised into "Ceylon Moors" and "Indian Moors".[64]

The Goan Muslims — a minority community who follow Islam in the western Indian coastal state of Goa — are commonly referred as *Moir* (Konkani: मैर) by Goan Catholics and Hindus.[a] *Moir* is derived from the Portuguese word *mouro* (Moor).

Moors of the Maghreb

In the late 7th and early 8th centuries CE, the Islamic Umayyad Caliphate, established after the death of Muhammad, underwent a period of rapid growth. In 647 CE, 40,000 Arabs forced the Byzantine governor of northern Africa to submit and pay tribute, but failed to permanently occupy the region.[65] After an interlude, during which the Muslims fought a civil war, the invasions resumed in 665, seizing Byzantine North Africa up to Bugia over the course of a series of campaigns, lasting until 689. A Byzantine counterattack largely expelled the Arabs but left the region vulnerable. Intermittent war over the inland provinces of North Africa continued for the next two decades. Further civil war delayed the continuation of further conquest, but an Arab assault took Carthage and held it against a Byzantine counterattack.

Figure 17: *The Great Mosque of Kairouan was founded by the Arab general Uqba ibn Nafi in 670 during the Islamic conquest, to provide a place of worship for recently converted or immigrating Muslims.*

Although a Christian and pagan Berber rebellion pushed out the Arabs temporarily, the Romanized urban population preferred the Arabs to the Berbers and welcomed a renewed and final conquest that left northern Africa in Muslim hands by 698. Over the next decades, the Berber and urban populations of northern Africa gradually converted to Islam, although for separate reasons.[66] The Arabic language was also adopted. Initially, the Arabs required only vassalage from the local inhabitants rather than assimilation, a process which took a considerable time. The groups that inhabited the Maghreb following this process became known collectively as Moors. Although the Berbers would later expel the Arabs from the Maghreb and form temporarily independent states, that effort failed to dislodge the usage of the collective term.

Moors of Iberia

In 711 the Islamic Arab and Moors of Berber descent in northern Africa crossed the Strait of Gibraltar onto the Iberian Peninsula, and in a series of raids they conquered Visigothic Christian Hispania. Their general, Tariq ibn Ziyad, brought most of Iberia under Islamic rule in an eight-year campaign. They continued northeast across the Pyrenees Mountains but were defeated by the Franks under Charles Martel at the Battle of Tours in 732.

Figure 18: *This is a large mural located on the ceiling of the Hall of Kings of the Alhambra which possibly depicts the first ten sultans of the Nasrid dynasty. It is a late-14th-century Gothic painting by a Christian Toledan artist.*

Figure 19: *Depiction of the Moors in Iberia, from The Cantigas de Santa Maria*

The Maghreb fell into a civil war in 739 that lasted until 743 known as the Berber Revolt. The Berbers revolted against the Umayyads, putting an end to Eastern dominion over the Maghreb. Despite racial tensions, Arabs and Berbers intermarried frequently. A few years later, the Eastern branch of the Umayyad dynasty was dethroned by the Abbasids and the Umayyad Caliphate overthrown in the Abbasid revolution (746-750). Abd al-Rahman I, who was of Arab-Berber lineage, managed to evade the Abbasids and flee to the Maghreb and then Iberia, where he founded the Emirate of Córdoba and the Andalusian branch of the Umayyad dynasty. The Moors ruled northern Africa and Al-Andalus for several centuries thereafter. Ibn Hazm, the polymath, mentions that many of the Caliphs in the Umayyad Caliphate and the Caliphate of Córdoba were blond and had light eyes. Ibn Hazm mentions that he preferred blondes, and notes that there was much interest in blondes in al-Andalus amongst the rulers and regular Muslims:

> *All the Caliphs of the Banu Marwan (God have mercy on their souls!), and especially the sons of al-Nasir, were without variation or exception disposed by nature to prefer blondes. I have myself seen them, and known others who had seen their forebears, from the days of al-Nasir's reign down to the present day; every one of them has been fair-haired, taking after their mothers, so that this has become a hereditary trait with them; all but Sulaiman al-Zafir (God have mercy on him!), whom I remember to have had black ringlets and a black beard. As for al-Nasir and al-Hakam al-Mustansir (may God be pleased with them!), I have been informed by my late father, the vizier, as well as by others, that both of them were blond and blue-eyed. The same is true of Hisham al-Mu'aiyad, Muhammad al-Mahdi, and 'Abd al-Rahman al-Murtada (may God be merciful to them all!); I saw them myself many times, and had the honour of being received by them, and I remarked that they all had fair hair and blue eyes.*[67]

The languages spoken in the parts of the Iberian Peninsula under Muslim rule were Andalusian Arabic and Mozarabic; they became extinct after the expulsion of the Moriscos, but Arabic language influence on the Spanish language can still be found today. The Muslims were resisted in parts of the Iberian Peninsula in areas of the northwest (such as Asturias, where they were defeated at the battle of Covadonga) and the largely Basque Country in the Pyrenees. Though the number of Moorish colonists was small, many native Iberian inhabitants converted to Islam. By 1000, according to Ronald Segal, some 5,000,000 of Iberia's 7,000,000 inhabitants, most of them descended from indigenous Iberian converts, were Muslim. There were also Sub-Saharan Africans who had been absorbed into al-Andalus to be used as soldiers and slaves. The Berber and Sub-Saharan African soldiers were known as "tangerines" because they were imported through Tangier.[68]

Figure 20: *Moorish army (right) of Almanzor during the Reconquista Battle of San Esteban de Gormaz, from Cantigas de Alfonso X el Sabio*

The Caliphate of Córdoba collapsed in 1031 and the Islamic territory in Iberia fell under the rule of the Almohad Caliphate in 1153. This second stage was guided by a version of Islam that left behind the more tolerant practices of the past.[69] Al-Andalus broke up into a number of taifas (fiefs), which were partly consolidated under the Caliphate of Córdoba.

The Kingdom of Asturias, a small northwestern Christian Iberian kingdom, initiated the *Reconquista* ("Reconquest") soon after the Islamic conquest in the 8th century. Christian states based in the north and west slowly extended their power over the rest of Iberia. The Kingdom of Navarre, the Kingdom of Galicia, the Kingdom of León, the Kingdom of Portugal, the Kingdom of Aragon, the *Marca Hispánica*, and the Crown of Castile began a process of expansion and internal consolidation during the next several centuries under the flag of Reconquista. In 1212, a coalition of Christian kings under the leadership of Alfonso VIII of Castile drove the Muslims from Central Iberia. The Portuguese side of the Reconquista ended in 1249 with the conquest of the Algarve (Arabic: الغرب – *al-Gharb*) under Afonso III. He was the first Portuguese monarch to claim the title "King of Portugal and the Algarve".

The Moorish Kingdom of Granada continued for three more centuries in southern Iberia. On 2 January 1492, the leader of the last Muslim stronghold

Figure 21: *A Moorish warrior embraces his Castilian ally during the Mudéjar revolt of 1264–66, taken from The Cantigas de Santa María*

in Granada surrendered to the armies of a recently united Christian Spain (after the marriage of Ferdinand II of Aragón and Isabella I of Castile, the "Catholic Monarchs"). The Moorish inhabitants received no military aid or rescue from other Muslim nations. The remaining Jews were also forced to leave Spain, convert to Roman Catholic Christianity, or be killed for refusing to do so. In 1480, to exert social and religious control, Isabella and Ferdinand agreed to allow the Inquisition in Spain. The Muslim population of Granada rebelled in 1499. The revolt lasted until early 1501, giving the Castilian authorities an excuse to void the terms of the Treaty of Granada (1491). In 1501, Castilian authorities delivered an ultimatum to the Muslims of Granada: they could either convert to Christianity or be expelled.

The Inquisition was aimed mostly at Jews and Muslims who had overtly converted to Christianity but were thought to be practicing their faiths secretly. They were respectively called *marranos* and *moriscos*. However, in 1567 King Philip II directed Moriscos to give up their Arabic names and traditional dress, and prohibited the use of Arabic. In reaction, there was a Morisco uprising in the Alpujarras from 1568 to 1571. In the years from 1609 to 1614, the government expelled Moriscos. The historian Henri Lapeyre estimated that this affected 300,000 out of an estimated total of 8 million inhabitants.[70]

Figure 22: *Court of the lions in the Alhambra, a Moorish palace built in the 14th century in Granada, Spain*

Some Muslims converted to Christianity and remained permanently in Iberia. This is indicated by a "high mean proportion of ancestry from North African (10.6%)" that "attests to a high level of religious conversion (whether voluntary or enforced), driven by historical episodes of social and religious intolerance, that ultimately led to the integration of descendants."[71,72] According to historian Richard A. Fletcher,[73] "the number of Arabs who settled in Iberia was very small. 'Moorish' Iberia does at least have the merit of reminding us that the bulk of the invaders and settlers were Moors, i.e., Berbers from Algeria and Morocco."

In the meantime, Spanish and Portuguese expeditions westward from the New World spread Christianity to India, the Malay peninsula, Indonesia, and the Philippines. By 1521, the ships of Magellan had reached that island archipelago, which they named *Las Islas Filipinas*, after Philip II of Spain. In Mindanao, the Spaniards named the kris-bearing people as Moros or 'Moors'. Today this ethnic group in Mindanao, who are generally Filipino Muslim, are called "Moros".

Figure 23: *Muslim musicians at the court of the Norman King Roger II of Sicily*

Moors of Sicily

The first Muslim conquest of Sicily began in 827, though it was not until 902 that almost the entire island was in the control of the Aghlabids, with the exception of some minor strongholds in the rugged interior. During that period some parts of southern Italy fell under Muslim control, most notably the port city of Bari, which formed the Emirate of Bari from 847-871. In 909, the Aghlabids was replaced by the Isma'ili rulers of the Fatimid Caliphate.Wikipedia:Citation needed Four years later, the Fatimid governor was ousted from Palermo when the island declared its independence under Emir Ahmed ibn-Kohrob. The language spoken in Sicily under Muslim rule was Siculo-Arabic.

In 1038, a Byzantine army under George Maniakes crossed the strait of Messina. This army included a corps of Normans that saved the situation in the first clash against the Muslims from Messina. After another decisive victory in the summer of 1040, Maniaces halted his march to lay siege to Syracuse. Despite his success, Maniaces was removed from his position, and the subsequent Muslim counter-offensive reconquered all the cities captured by the Byzantines.

The Norman Robert Guiscard, son of Tancred, invaded Sicily in 1060. The island was split between three Arab emirs, and the Christian population in many parts of the island rose up against the ruling Muslims. One year later, Messina

Figure 24: *Interior of the Mosque–Cathedral of Córdoba*

fell, and in 1072 Palermo was taken by the Normans. The loss of the cities, each with a splendid harbor, dealt a severe blow to Muslim power on the island. Eventually all of Sicily was taken. In 1091, Noto in the southern tip of Sicily and the island of Malta, the last Arab strongholds, fell to the Christians. Islamic authors noted the tolerance of the Norman kings of Sicily. Ali ibn al-Athir wrote: "They [the Muslims] were treated kindly, and they were protected, even against the Franks. Because of that, they had great love for King Roger."

The Muslim problem characterized Hohenstaufen rule in Sicily under Holy Roman Emperors Henry VI and his son, Frederick II. Many repressive measures were introduced by Frederick II to please the popes, who were intolerant of Islam in the heart of Christendom. This resulted in a rebellion by Sicilian Muslims, which in turn triggered organized resistance and systematic reprisals and marked the final chapter of Islam in Sicily. The complete eviction of Muslims and the annihilation of Islam in Sicily was completed by the late 1240s when the final deportations to Lucera took place.

Architecture

Moorish architecture is the articulated Islamic architecture of northern Africa and parts of Spain and Portugal, where the Moors were dominant between 711 and 1492. The best surviving examples of this architectural tradition are the Mosque–Cathedral of Córdoba and the Alhambra in Granada (mainly

Figure 25: *Coat of arms of Aragon with Moors' heads.*

1338–1390),[74] as well as the Giralda in Seville (1184).[75] Other notable examples include the ruined palace city of Medina Azahara (936–1010) and the Mosque of Cristo de la Luz, now a church, in Toledo, the Aljafería in Zaragoza and baths at for example Ronda and Alhama de Granada.

In heraldry

Moors—or more frequently their heads, often crowned—appear with some frequency in medieval European heraldry, though less so since the Middle Ages. The term ascribed to them in Anglo-Norman *blazon* (the language of English heraldry) is *maure*, though they are also sometimes called *moore*, *blackmoor*, *blackamoor* or *negro*. Maures appear in European heraldry from at least as early as the 13th century, and some have been attested as early as the 11th century in Italy, where they have persisted in the local heraldry and vexillology well into modern times in Corsica and Sardinia.

Armigers bearing moors or moors' heads may have adopted them for any of several reasons, to include symbolizing military victories in the Crusades, as a pun on the bearer's name in the canting arms of Morese, Negri, Saraceni, etc., or in the case of Frederick II, possibly to demonstrate the reach of his empire. The arms of Pope Benedict XVI feature a moor's head, crowned and

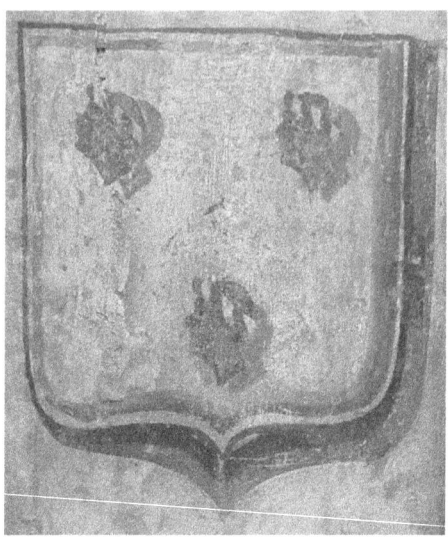

Figure 26: *Arms of the wealthy Bristol merchant and shipper William II Canynges (d.1474), as depicted on his canopied tomb in St Mary Redcliffe Church, showing the couped heads of three Moors wreathed at the temples*

Figure 27: *Flag of the Emirate of Granada of the Arab Nasrid dynasty, was the last Muslim kingdom of al-Andalus*

collared red, in reference to the arms of Freising, Germany. In the case of Corsica and Sardinia, the blindfolded moors' heads in the four quarters have long been said to represent the four Moorish emirs who were defeated by Peter I of Aragon and Pamplona in the 11th century, the four moors' heads around a cross having been adopted to the arms of Aragon around 1281–1387, and Corsica and Sardinia having come under the dominion of the king of Aragon in 1297. In Corsica, the blindfolds were lifted to the brow in the 18th century as a way of expressing the island's newfound independence.

Figure 28: *Moors on the North African coast, as depicted in Britain in 1739*

The use of Moors (and particularly their heads) as a heraldic symbol has been deprecated in modern North America.[76] For example, the College of Arms of the Society for Creative Anachronism urges applicants to use them delicately to avoid causing offence.

Population

Populations in Carthage circa 200 BC and northern Algeria 1500 BC were diverse.Wikipedia:Citation needed As a group, they plotted closest to the populations of Northern Egypt and intermediate to Northern Europeans and tropical Africans: "the data supported the comments from ancient authors observed by classicists: everything from fair-skinned blonds to peoples who were dark-skinned 'Ethiopian' or part Ethiopian in appearance."[77] Modern evidence shows a similar diversity among present North Africans. Moreover, this diversity of phenotypes and peoples was probably due to *in situ* differentiation, not foreign influxes.Wikipedia:Citation needed Foreign influxes are thought to have affected population make-up, but did not replace the indigenous Berber population.

As a large and diffuse ethnic group, the Moors consisted mostly of Berbers from Morocco and Western Algeria, sub-Saharan Africans from Mauritania, Northern Senegal, and Western Mali, Arab Bedouins, and Arab elite mostly

Figure 29: *Averroes, a Moorish polymath, was the founder of the Averroism school of philosophy, and influential in the rise of secular thought in Western Europe. Painted by Andrea Bonaiuto in 14th century*

from Yemen and Syria. Most writings on Moors applied darkness of skin as a trait for any and every Muslim invader of Europe.

In popular culture

- The title character in William Shakespeare's play *Othello*, and the derived title character in Verdi's opera *Otello*, is a Moor. The character has been played by various thespians in different forms of entertainment. A less well-known Moorish character, Aaron, appears in Shakespeare's earlier tragedy *Titus Andronicus*.
- Morgan Freeman's character Azeem in the 1991 film *Robin Hood: Prince of Thieves* is a Moor who Robin Hood saves from prison.
- The 2009 documentary film *Journey to Mecca* follows the travels of the Moorish explorer Ibn Battuta from his native country of Morocco to Mecca for the Hajj in 1325.

Notable Moors

- Tariq ibn Ziyad, Moorish general who defeated the Visigoths and conquered Hispania in 711.

- Abd ar-Rahman I, founder of the Umayyad Emirate of Córdoba in 756; along with its succeeding Caliphate of Córdoba, the dynasty ruled Islamic Iberia for three centuries.
- Ibn al-Qūṭiyya, Andalusian historian and grammarian.
- Yahya al-Laithi, Andalusian scholar who introduced the Maliki school of jurisprudence in Al-Andalus.
- Abbas ibn Firnas, 810–887, Berber inventor and aviator who invented an early parachute and made the first attempt at controlled flight with a hang glider.
- Maslama al-Majriti, died 1007, Andalusian writer believed to have been the author of the *Encyclopedia of the Brethren of Purity* and the *Picatrix*.
- Al-Zahrawi (Abulcasis), Andalusian physician and surgeon who established the discipline of surgery as a profession with his *Al-Tasrif* in 1000.
- Said Al-Andalusi, 1029–1070, Andalusian Qadi, historian, philosopher, mathematician and astronomer.
- Abū Ishāq Ibrāhīm al-Zarqālī (Arzachel), 1029–1087, Andalusian astronomer and engineer who developed the equatorium and universal (latitude-independent) astrolabe and compiled a *Zij* later used as a basis for the *Tables of Toledo*.
- Artephius, *circa* 1126, Andalusian scientist known as the author of numerous works of Alchemical texts, now extant only in Latin.
- Ibn Bajjah (Avempace), died 1138, Andalusian physicist and polymath whose theory of motion, including the concept of a reaction force, influenced the development of classical mechanics.
- Ibn Zuhr (Avenzoar), 1091–1161, Andalusian physician and polymath who discovered the existence of parasites and pioneered experimental surgery.
- Muhammad al-Idrisi, circa 1100–1166, Moorish geographer and polymath who drew the *Tabula Rogeriana*, the most accurate world map in pre-modern times.
- Ibn Tufail, circa 1105–1185, Arabic writer and polymath who wrote *Hayy ibn Yaqdhan*, the first philosophical novel.
- Averroes (Ibn Rushd), 1126–1198, classical Islamic philosopher and polymath who wrote *The Incoherence of the Incoherence* and the most extensive Aristotelian commentaries, and established the school of Averroism.
- Ibn al-Baitar, died 1248, Andalusian botanist and pharmacist who compiled the most extensive pharmacopoeia and botanical compilation in pre-modern times.
- Ibn Khaldun, a pioneer of the social sciences and forerunner of sociology, historiography and economics, who wrote the *Muqaddimah* in 1377.

- Abū al-Hasan ibn Alī al-Qalasādī, 1412–1486, Moorish mathematician who took the first steps toward the introduction of algebraic symbolism.
- Leo Africanus, 1494–1554, Andalusian geographer, author and diplomat, who was captured by Spanish pirates and sold as a slave, but later baptized and freed.
- Estevanico, also referred to as "Stephen the Moor", was an explorer in the service of Spain of what is now the southwest of the United States.
- Ibn Battuta, an Islamic scholar and Moorish explorer who is generally considered one of the greatest travellers of all time.
- Ibn Hazm, a Moorish polymath who was considered one of the leading thinkers of the Muslim World and is widely acknowledged as the father of Comparative religion studies.
- Ibn Idhari, a Moorish historian who was the author of (Al-Bayan al-Mughrib) an important medieval text on the history of the Maghreb and Iberia.

Ibn Arabi, Andalusian Sufi mystic and philosopher. Abu Bakr ibn al-Arabi **a judge and scholar of Maliki law from al-Andalus.**

Notes

<templatestyles src="Template:Refbegin/styles.css" />

- ˆ ...*Hindu Kristao **Moir** sogle bhau*- Hindus, Christians and Muslims are all brothers...

Bibliography

This section's bibliographical information is not fully provided. If you know these sources and can provide full information, you can help Wikipedia by completing it.

- Jan R. Carew. *Rape of Paradise: Columbus and the birth of racism in America*. Brooklyn, NY: A&B Books, c. 1994.
- David Brion Davis, "Slavery: White, Black, Muslim, Christian." *New York Review of Books*, vol. 48, #11 July 5, 2001. Do not have exact pages.
- Herodotus, *The Histories*
- Shomark O. Y. Keita, "Genetic Haplotypes in North Africa"
- Shomarka O. Y. Keita, "Studies of ancient crania from northern Africa." *American Journal of Physical Anthropology* 83:35-48 1990.
- Shomarka O. Y. Keita, "Further studies of crania from ancient northern Africa: an analysis of crania from First Dynasty Egyptian tombs, using multiple discriminant functions." *American Journal of Physical Anthropology* 87: 345-54, 1992.

- Shomarka O. Y. Keita, "Black Athena: race, Bernal and Snowden." *Arethusa* 26: 295-314, 1993.
- Bernard Lewis, "The Middle East".
- Bernard Lewis. *The Muslim Discovery of Europe*. NY: Norton, 1982. Also an article with the same title published in *Bulletin of the School of Oriental and African Studies*, University of London 20(1/3): 409-16, 1957.
- Bernard Lewis, "Race and Slavery in Islam".
- Stanley Lane-Poole, assisted by E. J. W. Gibb and Arthur Gilman. *The Story of Turkey*. NY: Putnam, 1888.
- Stanley Lane-Poole. *The Story of the Barbary Corsairs*. NY: Putnam,1890.
- Stanley Lane-Poole, *The History of the Moors in Spain.*
- J. A. (Joel Augustus) Rogers. *Nature Knows No Color Line: research into the Negro ancestry in the white race*. New York: 1952.
- Ronald Segal. *Islam's Black Slaves: the other Black diaspora*[78]. *NY: Farrar Straus Giroux, 2001.*
- Ivan Van Sertima, ed. The Golden Age of the Moor. New Brunswick: Transaction Publishers, 1992. (Journal of African civilizations, vol. 11).
- Frank Snowden. Before Color Prejudice: the ancient view of blacks. Cambridge, Massachusetts: Harvard Univ. Press, 1983.
- Frank Snowden. Blacks in antiquity: Ethiopians in the Greco-Roman experience. *Cambridge, Massachusetts: Belknap Press of Harvard University Press, 1970.*
- David M. Goldenberg. *The Curse of Ham: race and slavery in early Judaism, Christianity, and Islam*. Princeton, NJ: Princeton University Press, c2003.
- Lucotte and Mercier, various genetic studies
- Eva Borreguero. "The Moors Are Coming, the Moors Are Coming! Encounters with Muslims in Contemporary Spain." p. 417-32 in *Islam and Christian-Muslim Relations*, 2006, vol. 17, no. 4, pp. 417–32.

External links

Look up *Moor* or *Moorish* in Wiktionary, the free dictionary.

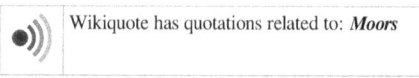
Wikiquote has quotations related to: *Moors*

Wikimedia Commons has media related to *Moors*.

- "The Moors" by Ross Brann, published on New York University website[79].
- Secret Seal: On the image of the Blackamoor in European Heraldry[80], a PBS article.
- Encyclopedia - Britannica Online Encyclopedia[81] (2006)
- Khalid Amine, Moroccan Shakespeare: From Moors to Moroccans[82]. Paper presented at an International Conference Organized by The Postgraduate School of Critical Theory and Cultural Studies, University of Nottingham, and The British Council, Morocco, 12–14 April 2001.
- Africans in Medieval & Renaissance Art: The Moor's Head[83], Victoria and Albert Museum (n.d)
- Sean Cavazos-Kottke. Othello's Predecessors: Moors in Renaissance Popular Literature[84]: (outline). Folger Shakespeare Library, 1998.

Al-Andalus

History of Al-Andalus
Muslim conquest (711–732)
• Battle of Guadalete • Battle of Toulouse • Battle of Tours
Umayyads of Córdoba (756–1031)
• Emirate of Córdoba • Caliphate of Córdoba • Al-Mansur Ibn Abi Aamir
First Taifa period (1009–1110)
Almoravid rule (1085–1145)
• Conquest • Battle of Sagrajas
Second Taifa period (1140–1203)
Almohad rule (1147–1238)
• Battle of Las Navas de Tolosa
Third Taifa period (1232–1287)
Emirate of Granada (1238–1492)
• Nasrid dynasty • Granada War
Related articles
• Iberia • Reconquista
• v • t • e[85]

Al-Andalus (Arabic: الأَنْدَلُس, trans. *al-'Andalus*; Spanish: *al-Ándalus*; Portuguese: *al-Ândalus*; Catalan: *al-Àndalus*; Berber: *Andalus*), also known as **Muslim Spain**, **Muslim Iberia**, or **Islamic Iberia**, was a medieval Muslim territory and cultural domain that in its early period occupied most of Iberia, today's Portugal and Spain. At its greatest geographical extent in the early 8th century, it briefly occupied a part of present day southern France Septimania, and the northwest of the Iberian peninsula. The name more generally describes the parts of the peninsula governed by Muslims (given the generic

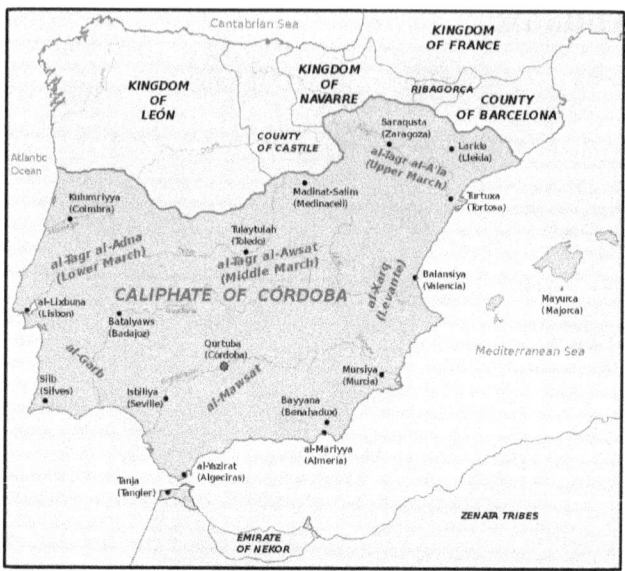

Figure 30: *Al-Andalus and Christian kingdoms circa 1000 AD, at the apogee of Almanzor*

name of Moors) at various times between 711 and 1492, though the boundaries changed constantly as the Christian Reconquista progressed,[86] eventually shrinking to the south around modern-day Andalusia and then to the Emirate of Granada.

Following the Umayyad conquest of Hispania, al-Andalus, then at its greatest extent, was divided into five administrative units, corresponding roughly to modern Andalusia, Portugal and Galicia, Castile and León, Navarre, Aragon, the County of Barcelona, and Septimania.[87] As a political domain, it successively constituted a province of the Umayyad Caliphate, initiated by the Caliph Al-Walid I (711–750); the Emirate of Córdoba (c. 750–929); the Caliphate of Córdoba (929–1031); and the Caliphate of Córdoba's *taifa* (successor) kingdoms. Rule under these kingdoms led to a rise in cultural exchange and cooperation between Muslims and Christians. Christians and Jews were subject to a special tax called Jizya, to the state, which in return provided internal autonomy in practicing their religion and offered the same level of protections by the Muslim rulers.[88]

Under the Caliphate of Córdoba, al-Andalus was a beacon of learning, and the city of Córdoba, the largest in Europe, became one of the leading cultural and economic centres throughout the Mediterranean Basin, Europe, and the Islamic world. Achievements that advanced Islamic and Western science came from al-Andalus, including major advances in trigonometry (Geber), astronomy (Arzachel), surgery (Abulcasis), pharmacology (Avenzoar), agronomy (Ibn Bassal and Abū l-Khayr al-Ishbīlī), and other fields. Al-Andalus became a major educational center for Europe and the lands around the Mediterranean Sea as well as a conduit for culture and science between the Islamic and Christian worlds.

For much of its history, al-Andalus existed in conflict with Christian kingdoms to the north. After the fall of the Umayyad caliphate, al-Andalus was fragmented into minor states and principalities. Attacks from the Christians intensified, led by the Castilians under Alfonso VI. The Almoravid empire intervened and repelled the Christian attacks on the region, deposing the weak Andalusi Muslim princes and included al-Andalus under direct Berber rule. In the next century and a half, al-Andalus became a province of the Berber Muslim empires of the Almoravids and Almohads, both based in Marrakesh.

Ultimately, the Christian kingdoms in the north of the Iberian Peninsula overpowered the Muslim states to the south. In 1085, Alfonso VI captured Toledo, starting a gradual decline of Muslim power. With the fall of Córdoba in 1236, most of the south quickly fell under Christian rule and the Emirate of Granada became a tributary state of the Kingdom of Castile two years later. In 1249, the Portuguese Reconquista culminated with the conquest of the Algarve by Afonso III, leaving Granada as the last Muslim state on the Iberian Peninsula. Finally, on January 2, 1492, Emir Muhammad XII surrendered the Emirate of Granada to Queen Isabella I of Castile, completing the Christian Reconquista of the peninsula. Although al-Andalus ended as a political entity, the nearly eight centuries of Islamic rule which preceded and accompanied the early formation of the Spanish nation-state and identity has left a profound effect on the country's culture and language, particularly in Andalusia.

Name

The toponym *al-Andalus* is first attested by inscriptions on coins minted in 716 by the new Muslim government of Iberia. These coins, called *dinars*, were inscribed in both Latin and Arabic. The etymology of the name *"al-Andalus"* has traditionally been derived from the name of the *Vandals*; however, proposals since the 1980s have challenged this contention. In 1986, Joaquín Vallvé proposed that *"al-Andalus"* was a corruption of the name *Atlantis*, Halm in 1989 derived the name from a Gothic term, **landahlauts*, and in 2002, Bossong suggested its derivation from a pre-Roman substrate.

Figure 31:
The Age of the Caliphs
Muhammad, 622–632
Rashidun Caliphate, 632–661
Umayyad Caliphate, 661–750

History

Province of the Umayyad Caliphate

During the caliphate of the Umayyad Caliph Al-Walid I, the commander Tariq ibn-Ziyad led a small force that landed at Gibraltar on April 30, 711, ostensibly to intervene in a Visigothic civil war. After a decisive victory over King Roderic at the Battle of Guadalete on July 19, 711, Tariq ibn-Ziyad, joined by Arab governor Musa ibn Nusayr of Ifriqiya, brought most of the Visigothic Kingdom under Muslim occupation in a seven-year campaign. They crossed the Pyrenees and occupied Visigothic Septimania in southern France.

Most of the Iberian peninsula became part of the expanding Umayyad Empire, under the name of *al-Andalus*. It was organized as a province subordinate to Ifriqiya, so, for the first few decades, the governors of al-Andalus were appointed by the emir of Kairouan, rather than the Caliph in Damascus. The regional capital was set at Córdoba, and the first influx of Muslim settlers was widely distributed.

The small army Tariq led in the initial conquest consisted mostly of Berbers, while Musa's largely Arab force of over 12,000 soldiers was accompanied by a group of *mawālī* (Arabic, موالي), that is, non-Arab Muslims, who were clients of the Arabs. The Berber soldiers accompanying Tariq were garrisoned in the centre and the north of the peninsula, as well as in the Pyrenees, while the Berber colonists who followed settled in all parts of the country – north, east, south and west. Visigothic lords who agreed to recognize Muslim suzerainty

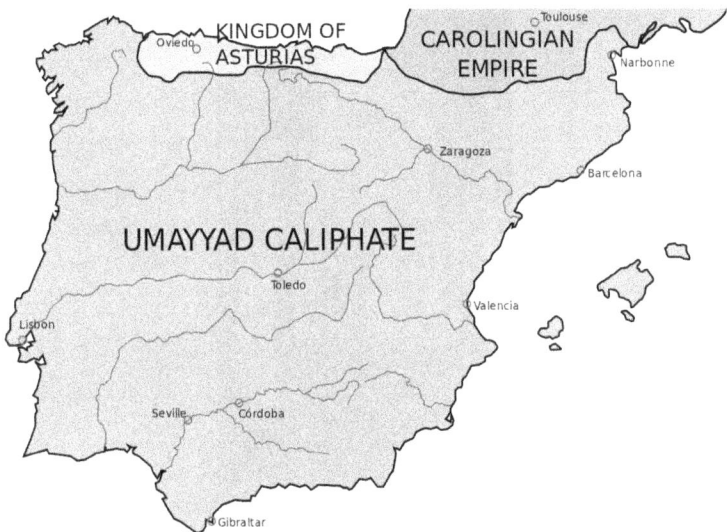

Figure 32: *The province of al-Andalus in 750*

were allowed to retain their fiefs (notably, in Murcia, Galicia, and the Ebro valley). Resistant Visigoths took refuge in the Cantabrian highlands, where they carved out a rump state, the Kingdom of Asturias.

In the 720s, the al-Andalus governors launched several *sa'ifa* raids into Aquitaine, but were severely defeated by Duke Odo the Great of Aquitaine at the Battle of Toulouse (721). However, after crushing Odo's Berber ally Uthman ibn Naissa on the eastern Pyrenees, Abdul Rahman Al Ghafiqi led an expedition north across the western Pyrenees and defeated the Aquitanian duke, who in turn appealed to the Frankish leader Charles Martel for assistance, offering to place himself under Carolingian sovereignty. At the Battle of Poitiers in 732, the al-Andalus raiding army was defeated by Charles Martel. In 734, the Andalusi launched raids to the east, capturing Avignon and Arles and overran much of Provence. In 737, they traveled up the Rhône valley, reaching as far north as Burgundy. Charles Martel of the Franks, with the assistance of Liutprand of the Lombards, invaded Burgundy and Provence and expelled the raiders by 739.

Relations between Arabs and Berbers in al-Andalus had been tense in the years after the conquest. Berbers heavily outnumbered the Arabs in the province, had done the bulk of the fighting, and were assigned the harsher duties (e.g. garrisoning the more troubled areas). Although some Arab governors had cultivated their Berber lieutenants, others had grievously mistreated them. Mutinies by Berber soldiers were frequent; e.g., in 729, the Berber commander

Figure 33: *Interior of the Mosque–Cathedral of Córdoba formerly the Great Mosque of Córdoba. The original mosque (742), since much enlarged, was built on the site of the Visigothic Christian 'Saint Vincent basilica' (600).*

Munnus had revolted and managed to carve out a rebel state in Cerdanya for a while.

In 740, a Berber Revolt erupted in the Maghreb (North Africa). To put down the rebellion, the Umayyad Caliph Hisham dispatched a large Arab army, composed of regiments (*Junds*) of Bilad Ash-Sham,[89] to North Africa. But the great Syrian army was crushed by the Berber rebels at the Battle of Bagdoura (in Morocco). Heartened by the victories of their North African brethren, the Berbers of al-Andalus quickly raised their own revolt. Berber garrisons in northern Spain mutinied, deposed their Arab commanders, and organized a large rebel army to march against the strongholds of Toledo, Cordoba, and Algeciras.

In 741, Balj b. Bishr led a detachment of some 10,000 of the Arabic-speaking troops referred to as "the Syrians" across the straits. The Arab governor of al-Andalus, joined by this force, crushed the Berber rebels in a series of ferocious battles in 742. However, a quarrel immediately erupted between the Syrian commanders and the Andalusi, the so-called "original Arabs" of the earlier contingents. The Syrians defeated them at the hard-fought Battle of Aqua Portora in August 742 but were too few to impose themselves on the province.

Figure 34: *Portrait of Abd al-Rahman I*

The quarrel was settled in 743 when Abū l-Khaṭṭār al-Ḥusām, the new governor of al-Andalus, assigned the Syrians to regimental fiefs across al-Andalus – the Damascus jund was established in Elvira (Granada), the Jordan jund in Rayyu (Málaga and Archidona), the Jund Filastin in Medina-Sidonia and Jerez, the Emesa (Hims) jund in Seville and Niebla, and the Qinnasrin jund in Jaén. The Egypt jund was divided between Beja (Alentejo) in the west and Tudmir (Murcia) in the east.[90] The arrival of the Syrians substantially increased the Arab element in the Iberian peninsula and helped strengthen the Muslim hold on the south. However, at the same time, unwilling to be governed, the Syrian *junds* carried on an existence of autonomous feudal anarchy, severely destabilizing the authority of the governor of al-Andalus.

A second significant consequence of the revolt was the expansion of the Kingdom of the Asturias, hitherto confined to enclaves in the Cantabrian highlands. After the rebellious Berber garrisons evacuated the northern frontier fortresses, the Christian king Alfonso I of Asturias set about immediately seizing the empty forts for himself, quickly adding the northwestern provinces of Galicia and León to his fledgling kingdom. The Asturians evacuated the Christian populations from the towns and villages of the Galician-Leonese lowlands, creating an empty buffer zone in the Douro River valley (the "Desert of the Duero"). This newly emptied frontier remained roughly in place for the next few centuries as the boundary between the Christian north and the Islamic south. Between this frontier and its heartland in the south, the al-Andalus state had three large march territories (*thughur*): the Lower March (capital initially at Mérida, later Badajoz), the Middle March (centered at Toledo), and the Upper March (centered at Zaragoza).

These disturbances and disorders also allowed the Franks, now under the leadership of Pepin the Short, to invade the strategic strip of Septimania in 752, hoping to deprive al-Andalus of an easy launching pad for raids into Francia. After a lengthy siege, the last Arab stronghold, the citadel of Narbonne, finally fell to the Franks in 759. Al-Andalus was sealed off at the Pyrenees.[91]

The third consequence of the Berber revolt was the collapse of the authority of the Damascus Caliphate over the western provinces. With the Umayyad Caliphs distracted by the challenge of the Abbasids in the east, the western provinces of the Maghreb and al-Andalus spun out of their control. From around 745, the Fihrids, an illustrious local Arab clan descended from Oqba ibn Nafi al-Fihri, seized power in the western provinces and ruled them almost as a private family empire of their own – Abd al-Rahman ibn Habib al-Fihri in Ifriqiya and Yūsuf al-Fihri in al-Andalus. The Fihrids welcomed the fall of the Umayyads in the east, in 750, and sought to reach an understanding with the Abbasids, hoping they might be allowed to continue their autonomous existence. But when the Abbasids rejected the offer and demanded submission, the Fihrids declared independence and, probably out of spite, invited the deposed remnants of the Umayyad clan to take refuge in their dominions. It was a fateful decision that they soon regretted, for the Umayyads, the sons and grandsons of caliphs, had a more legitimate claim to rule than the Fihrids themselves. Rebellious-minded local lords, disenchanted with the autocratic rule of the Fihrids, conspired with the arriving Umayyad exiles.

Umayyad Emirate and Caliphate of Córdoba

In 756, the exiled Umayyad prince Abd al-Rahman I (nicknamed *al-Dākhil*, the 'Immigrant') ousted Yūsuf al-Fihri to establish himself as the Emir of Córdoba. He refused to submit to the Abbasid caliph, as Abbasid forces had killed most of his family. Over a thirty-year reign, he established a tenuous rule over much of al-Andalus, overcoming partisans of both the al-Fihri family and of the Abbasid caliph.[92]

For the next century and a half, his descendants continued as emirs of Córdoba with nominal control over the rest of al-Andalus and sometimes parts of western North Africa, but with real control, particularly over the marches along the Christian border, vacillating depending on the competence of the individual emir. Indeed, the power of emir Abdallah ibn Muhammad (circa 900) did not extend beyond Córdoba itself. But his grandson Abd-al-Rahman III, who

Figure 35: *Abd-ar-Rahman III and his court receiving an ambassador in Medina Azahara, Còrdoba*

succeeded him in 912, not only rapidly restored Umayyad power throughout al-Andalus but extended it into western North Africa as well. In 929 he proclaimed himself Caliph, elevating the emirate to a position competing in prestige not only with the Abbasid caliph in Baghdad but also the Fatimid caliph in Tunis—with whom he was competing for control of North Africa.

The period of the Caliphate is seen as the golden age of al-Andalus. Crops produced using irrigation, along with food imported from the Middle East, provided the area around Córdoba and some other *Andalusī* cities with an agricultural economic sector that was the most advanced in Europe by far, sparking the Arab Agricultural Revolution. Among European cities, Córdoba under the Caliphate, with a population of perhaps 500,000, eventually overtook Constantinople as the largest and most prosperous city in Europe.[93] Within the Islamic world, Córdoba was one of the leading cultural centres. The work of its most important philosophers and scientists (notably Abulcasis and Averroes) had a major influence on the intellectual life of medieval Europe.

Muslims and non-Muslims often came from abroad to study in the famous libraries and universities of al-Andalus, mainly after the reconquest of Toledo in 1085 and the establishment of translation institutions such as the Toledo School of Translators. The most noted of those was Michael Scot (c. 1175 to c. 1235), who took the works of Ibn Rushd ("Averroes") and Ibn Sina ("Avicenna") to Italy. This transmission of ideas remains one of the greatest in history, significantly affecting the formation of the European Renaissance.[94]

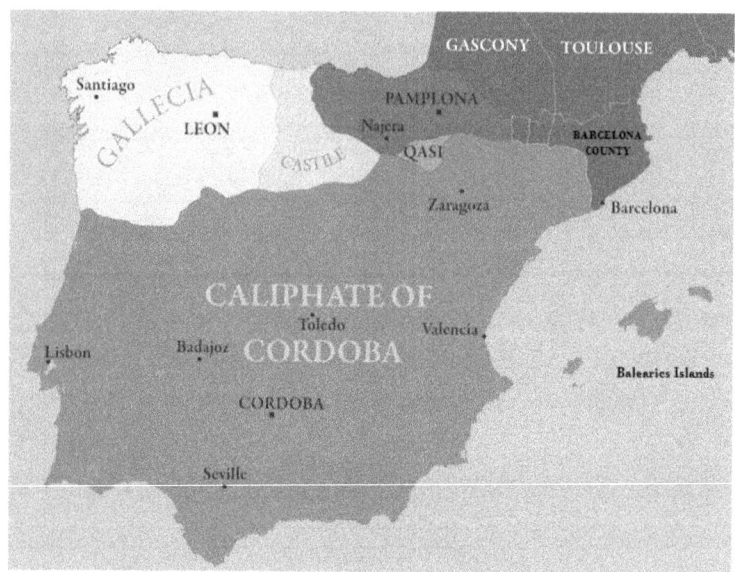

Figure 36: *The Caliphate of Cordoba in the early 10th century*

Figure 37: *Gold dinar minted in Córdoba during the reign of Hisham II*

Taifas period

The Caliphate of Córdoba effectively collapsed during a ruinous civil war between 1009 and 1013, although it was not finally abolished until 1031 when *al-Andalus* broke up into a number of mostly independent mini-states and principalities called *taifas*. In 1013, invading Berbers sacked Córdoba, massacring its inhabitants, pillaging the city, and burning the palace complex to

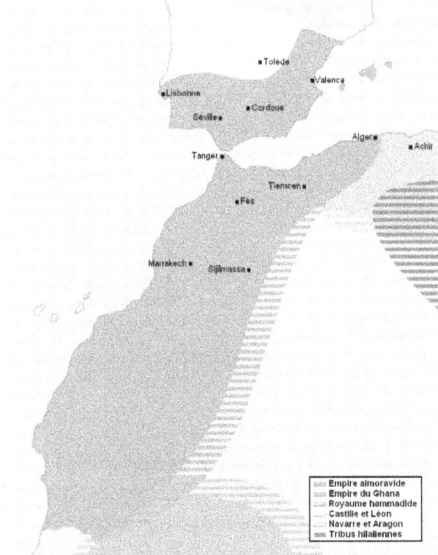

Figure 38: *Map showing the extent of the Almoravid empire*

the ground. After 1031, the *taifas* were generally too weak to defend themselves against repeated raids and demands for tribute from the Christian states to the north and west, which were known to the Muslims as "the Galician nations",[95] and which had spread from their initial strongholds in Galicia, Asturias, Cantabria, the Basque country, and the Carolingian *Marca Hispanica* to become the Kingdoms of Navarre, León, Portugal, Castile and Aragon, and the County of Barcelona. Eventually raids turned into conquests, and in response the *Taifa* kings were forced to request help from the Almoravids, Muslim Berber rulers of the Maghreb. Their desperate maneuver would eventually fall to their disadvantage, however, as the Almoravids they had summoned from the south went on to conquer and annex all the *Taifa* kingdoms.

Almoravids, Almohads, and Marinids

In 1086 the Almoravid ruler of Morocco, Yusuf ibn Tashfin, was invited by the Muslim princes in Iberia to defend them against Alfonso VI, King of Castile and León. In that year, Tashfin crossed the straits to Algeciras and inflicted a severe defeat on the Christians at the Battle of Sagrajas. By 1094, ibn Tashfin had removed all Muslim princes in Iberia and had annexed their states, except for the one at Zaragoza. He also regained Valencia from the Christians.

The Almoravids were succeeded by the Almohads, another Berber dynasty, after the victory of Abu Yusuf Ya'qub al-Mansur over the Castilian Alfonso VIII

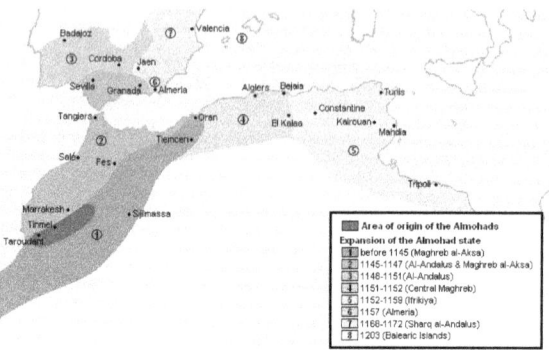

Figure 39: *Expansion of the Almohad state in the 12th century*

at the Battle of Alarcos in 1195. In 1212, a coalition of Christian kings under the leadership of the Castilian Alfonso VIII defeated the Almohads at the Battle of Las Navas de Tolosa. The Almohads continued to rule Al-Andalus for another decade, though with much reduced power and prestige. The civil wars following the death of Abu Ya'qub Yusuf II rapidly led to the re-establishment of taifas. The taifas, newly independent but now weakened, were quickly conquered by Portugal, Castile, and Aragon. After the fall of Murcia (1243) and the Algarve (1249), only the Emirate of Granada survived as a Muslim state, and only as a tributary of Castile until 1492. Most of its tribute was paid in gold that was carried to Iberia from present-day Mali and Burkina Faso through the merchant routes of the Sahara.

The last Muslim threat to the Christian kingdoms was the rise of the Marinids in Morocco during the 14th century. They took Granada into their sphere of influence and occupied some of its cities, like Algeciras. However, they were unable to take Tarifa, which held out until the arrival of the Castilian Army led by Alfonso XI. The Castilian king, with the help of Afonso IV of Portugal and Peter IV of Aragon, decisively defeated the Marinids at the Battle of Río Salado in 1340 and took Algeciras in 1344. Gibraltar, then under Granadian rule, was besieged in 1349–50. Alfonso XI and most of his army perished by the Black Death. His successor, Peter of Castile, made peace with the Muslims and turned his attention to Christian lands, starting a period of almost 150 years of rebellions and wars between the Christian states that secured the survival of Granada.

Figure 40: *A painting of Muhammad XII of Granada, last Muslim sultan in Spain. Date of this painting and its current location are unknown.*

Emirate of Granada, its fall, and aftermath

From the mid 13th to the late 15th century, the only remaining domain of al-Andalus was the Emirate of Granada, the last Muslim stronghold in the Iberian Peninsula. The emirate was established by Muhammad ibn al-Ahmar in 1230 and was ruled by the Nasrid dynasty, the longest reigning dynasty in the history of al-Andalus. Although surrounded by Castilian lands, the emirate was wealthy through being tightly integrated in Mediterranean trade networks and enjoyed a period of considerable cultural and economic prosperity. However, for most of its existence Granada was a tributary state, with Nasrid emirs paying tribute to Castilian kings. Granada's status as a tributary state and its favorable geographic location, with the Sierra Nevada as a natural barrier, helped to prolong Nasrid rule and allowed the emirate to prosper as a regional entrepôt with the Maghreb and the rest of Africa. The city of Granada also served as a refuge for Muslims fleeing during the Reconquista, accepting numerous Muslims expelled from Christian controlled areas, doubling the size of the city[96] and even becoming one of the largest in Europe throughout the 15th century in terms of population.

In 1469, the marriage of Ferdinand of Aragon and Isabella of Castile signaled the launch of the final assault on the emirate. The King and Queen convinced

Figure 41: *Muhammad XII's family in the Alhambra moments after the fall of Granada, by Manuel Gómez-Moreno González, c. 1880*

Pope Sixtus IV to declare their war a crusade. The Catholic Monarchs crushed one center of resistance after another until finally on January 2, 1492, after a long siege, the emirate's last sultan Muhammad XII surrendered the city and the fortress palace, the renowned Alhambra (see Fall of Granada).

By this time Muslims in Castile numbered half a million. After the fall, "100,000 had died or been enslaved, 200,000 emigrated, and 200,000 remained as the residual population. Many of the Muslim elite, including Muhammad XII, who had been given the area of the Alpujarras mountains as a principality, found life under Christian rule intolerable and passed over into North Africa." Under the conditions of the Capitulations of 1492, the Muslims in Granada were to be allowed to continue to practice their religion.

Mass forced conversions of Muslims in 1499 led to a revolt that spread to Alpujarras and the mountains of Ronda; after this uprising the capitulations were revoked. In 1502 the Catholic Monarchs decreed the forced conversion of all Muslims living under the rule of the Crown of Castile, although in the kingdoms of Aragon and Valencia (both now part of Spain) the open practice of Islam was allowed until 1526. Descendants of the Muslims were subject to expulsions from Spain between 1609 and 1614 (see Expulsion of the Moriscos).[97] The last mass prosecution against Moriscos for crypto-Islamic

Al-Andalus

Figure 42: *Clothing of al-Andalus in the 15th century, during the Emirate of Granada*

practices occurred in Granada in 1727, with most of those convicted receiving relatively light sentences. From then on, indigenous Islam is considered to have been extinguished in Spain.[98]

Society

The society of al-Andalus was made up of three main religious groups: Muslims, Christians, and Jews. The Muslims, although united on the religious level, had several ethnic divisions, the main being the distinction between the Arabs and the Berbers. The Arab elite regarded non-Arab Muslims as second-class citizens; and they were particularly scornful of the Berbers.

The ethnic structure of al-Andalus consisted of Arabs at the top of the social scale followed by, in descending order, Berbers, Muladies, Mozarabes, and Jews. Each of these communities inhabited distinct neighborhoods in the cities. In the 10th century a massive conversion of Christians took place, and *muladies* (Muslims of native Iberian origin), formed the majority of Muslims. The Muladies had spoken in a Romance dialect of Latin called Mozarabic while increasingly adopting the Arabic language, which eventually evolved into the Andalusi Arabic in which Muslims, Jews, and Christians became monolingual in the last surviving Muslim state in the Iberian Peninsula, the Emirate of

Figure 43: *A Christian and a Muslim playing chess in 13th-century al-Andalus*

Granada (1230-1492). Eventually, the Muladies, and later the Berber tribes, adopted an Arabic identity like the majority of subject people in Egypt, the Levant, Mesopotamia, and North Africa. Muladies, together with other Muslims, comprised eighty percent of the population of al-Andalus by 1100.[99,100] Mozarabs were Christians who had long lived under Muslim and Arab rule, adopting many Arab customs, art, and words, while still maintaining their Christian and Latin rituals and their own Romance languages.

The Jewish population worked mainly as tax collectors, in trade, or as doctors or ambassadors. At the end of the 15th century there were about 50,000 Jews in Granada and roughly 100,000 in the whole of Islamic Iberia.[101]

Non-Muslims under the Caliphate

Non-Muslims were given the status of *ahl al-dhimma* (the people under protection), with adult men paying a "Jizya" tax, equal to one dinar per year with exemptions for the elderly and the disabled. Those who were neither Christians nor Jews, such as pagans, were given the status of *Majus*.[102] The treatment of non-Muslims in the Caliphate has been a subject of considerable debate among scholars and commentators, especially those interested in drawing parallels to the coexistence of Muslims and non-Muslims in the modern world.

Jews constituted more than five percent of the population. Al-Andalus was a key centre of Jewish life during the early Middle Ages, producing important scholars and one of the most stable and wealthy Jewish communities.

Al-Andalus

Figure 44: *Image of a Jewish cantor reading the Passover story in al-Andalus, from a 14th-century Spanish Haggadah*

The longest period of relative tolerance began after 912 with the reign of Abd-ar-Rahman III and his son, Al-Hakam II, when the Jews of al-Andalus prospered, devoting themselves to the service of the Caliphate of Córdoba, to the study of the sciences, and to commerce and industry, especially trading in silk and slaves, in this way promoting the prosperity of the country. Southern Iberia became an asylum for the oppressed Jews of other countries.[103,104]

Under the Almoravids and the Almohads there may have been intermittent persecution of Jews,[105] but sources are extremely scarce and do not give a clear picture, though the situation appears to have deteriorated after 1160.[106] Muslim pogroms against Jews in al-Andalus occurred in Córdoba (1011) and in Granada (1066).[107,108,109] However, massacres of *dhimmis* are rare in Islamic history.

The Almohads, who had taken control of the Almoravids' Maghribi and Andalusi territories by 1147,[110] far surpassed the Almoravides in fundamentalist outlook, and they treated the non-Muslims harshly. Faced with the choice of either death or conversion, many Jews and Christians emigrated.[111] Some, such as the family of Maimonides, fled east to more tolerant Muslim lands.

Figure 45: *The Alhambra, constructed by the orders of the first Nasrid emir Ibn al-Ahmar in the 13th century*

Culture

Many ethnicities, religions, and races coexisted in al-Andalus, each contributing to its intellectual prosperity. Literacy in Islamic Iberia was far more widespread than in many other nations in the West at the time.[112]

From the earliest days, the Umayyads wanted to be seen as intellectual rivals to the Abbasids, and for Córdoba to have libraries and educational institutions to rival Baghdad's. Although there was a clear rivalry between the two powers, there was freedom to travel between the two caliphates,Wikipedia:Citation needed which helped spread new ideas and innovations over time.

Art and architecture

The Alhambra palace and fortress best reflects the culture and art of the last centuries of Moorish rule of Al-Andalus. The complex was completed towards the end of the Muslim rule of Spain by Yusuf I (1333–1353) and Muhammed V, Sultan of Granada (1353–1391). Artists and intellectuals took refuge at Alhambra after the Reconquista began to roll back Muslim territory. The site integrates natural qualities with constructed structures and gardens, and is a testament to Moorish culture in Spain and to the skills of the Muslim artisans, craftsmen, and builders of their era.

The decoration within the palace comes from the last great period of Andalusian art in Granada, with little of the Byzantine influence of contemporary Abbasid architecture. Artists endlessly reproduced the same forms and trends, creating a new style that developed over the course of the Nasrid Dynasty using elements created and developed during the centuries of Muslim rule on the Peninsula, including the Caliphate horseshoe arch, the Almohad sebka (a grid of rhombuses), the Almoravid palm, and unique combinations of these, as well as innovations such as stilted arches and muqarnas (stalactite ceiling decorations). Columns and muqarnas appear in several chambers, and the interiors of numerous palaces are decorated with arabesques and calligraphy. The arabesques of the interior are ascribed to, among other sultans, Yusuf I, Muhammed V, and Ismail I, Sultan of Granada.

Philosophy

Al-Andalus philosophy

The historian Said al-Andalusi wrote that Caliph Abd-ar-Rahman III had collected libraries of books and granted patronage to scholars of medicine and "ancient sciences". Later, *al-Mustansir* (Al-Hakam II) went yet further, building a university and libraries in Córdoba. Córdoba became one of the world's leading centres of medicine and philosophical debate.

When Al-Hakam's son Hisham II took over, real power was ceded to the *hajib*, al-Mansur Ibn Abi Aamir. Al-Mansur was a distinctly religious man and disapproved of the sciences of astronomy, logic, and especially of astrology, so much so that many books on these subjects, which had been preserved and collected at great expense by Al-Hakam II, were burned publicly. With Al-Mansur's death in 1002, interest in philosophy revived. Numerous scholars emerged, including Abu Uthman Ibn Fathun, whose masterwork was the philosophical treatise "Tree of Wisdom". Maslamah Ibn Ahmad al-Majriti (died 1008) was an outstanding scholar in astronomy and astrology; he was an intrepid traveller who journeyed all over the Islamic world and beyond and kept in touch with the Brethren of Purity. He is said to have brought the 51 "Epistles of the Brethren of Purity" to *al-Andalus* and added the compendium to this work, although it is quite possible that it was added later by another scholar with the name al-Majriti. Another book attributed to al-Majriti is the *Ghayat al-Hakim*, "The Aim of the Sage", which explored a synthesis of Platonism with Hermetic philosophy. Its use of incantations led the book to be widely dismissed in later years, although the Sufi communities continued to study it.

A prominent follower of al-Majriti was the philosopher and geometer Abu al-Hakam al-Kirmani who was followed, in turn, by Abu Bakr Ibn al-Sayigh, usually known in the Arab world as Ibn Bajjah, "Avempace".

Figure 46: *Averroes, founder of the Averroism school of philosophy, was influential in the rise of secular thought in Western Europe. Detail from Triunfo de Santo Tomás by Andrea Bonaiuto, 14th century*

The al-Andalus philosopher Averroes (1126–1198) was the founder of the Averroism school of philosophy, and his works and commentaries influenced medieval thought in Western EuropeWikipedia:Citation needed. Another influential al-Andalus philosopher was Ibn Tufail.

Jewish philosophy and culture

As Jewish thought in Babylonia declined, the tolerance of *al-Andalus* made it the new centre of Jewish intellectual endeavours. Poets and commentators like Judah Halevi (1086–1145) and Dunash ben Labrat (920–990) contributed to the cultural life of *al-Andalus*, but the area was even more important to the development of Jewish philosophy. A stream of Jewish philosophers, cross-fertilizing with Muslim philosophers (see joint Jewish and Islamic philosophies), culminated with the widely celebrated Jewish thinker of the Middle Ages, Maimonides (1135–1205), though he did not actually do any of his work in *al-Andalus*, his family having fled persecution by the Almohads when he was 13.

Figure 47: *Jewish Street Sign in Toledo, Spain*

Homosexuality

In the book *Medieval Iberia: An Encyclopedia* Daniel Eisenberg describes homosexuality as "a key symbolic issue throughout the Middle Ages in Iberia", stating that "in al-Andalus homosexual pleasures were much indulged in by the intellectual and political elite. Evidence includes the behaviour of rulers, such as Abd al-Rahmn III, Al-Hakam II, Hisham II, and Al Mu'tamid, who openly kept male harems; the memoirs of Abdallah ibn Buluggin, last Zirid king of Granada, makes references to male prostitutes, who charged higher fees and had a higher class of clientele than did their female counter-parts: the repeated criticisms of Christians; and especially the abundant poetry. Both pederasty and love between adult males are found. Although homosexual practices were never officially condoned, prohibitions against them were rarely enforced, and usually there was not even a pretense of doing so." Male homosexual relations allowed nonprocreative sexual practices and were not seen as a form of identity. Very little is known about the homosexual behaviour of women.

References

- Glick, Thomas (1999). "Islamic and Christian Spain in the Early Middle Ages: Comparative Perspectives on Social and Cultural Formation"[113]. Retrieved 23 October 2011.Wikipedia:Link rot

Bibliography

- Alfonso, Esperanza, 2007. *Islamic Culture Through Jewish Eyes: al-Andalus from the Tenth to Twelfth Century*. NY: Routledge. ISBN 978-0-415-43732-5
- Al-Djazairi, Salah Eddine 2005. *The Hidden Debt to Islamic Civilisation*. Manchester: Bayt Al-Hikma Press. ISBN 0-9551156-1-2
- Bossong, Georg. 2002. "Der Name *Al-Andalus*: Neue Überlegungen zu einem alten Problem", *Sounds and Systems: Studies in Structure and Change. A Festschrift for Theo Vennemann*, eds. David Restle & Dietmar Zaefferer. Berlin: Mouton de Gruyter, pp. 149–164. (In German) Also available online: see External Links below.
- Cohen, Mark. 1994. *Under Crescent and Cross: The Jews in the Middle Ages*. Princeton, NJ: Princeton University Press. ISBN 0-691-01082-X
- Collins, Roger. 1989. *The Arab Conquest of Spain, 710–797*, Oxford: Blackwell. ISBN 0-631-19405-3
- Dodds, Jerrilynn D. (1992). *Al-Andalus: the art of Islamic Spain*[114]. New York: The Metropolitan Museum of Art. ISBN 9780870996368.
- Fernandez-Morera, Dario. 2016. *The Myth of the Andalusian Paradise: Muslims, Christians, and Jews under Islamic Rule in Medieval Spain*. NY: Intercollegiate Studies Institute. ISBN 978-1610170956
- Frank, Daniel H. & Leaman, Oliver. 2003. *The Cambridge Companion to Medieval Jewish Philosophy*. Cambridge: Cambridge University Press. ISBN 0-521-65574-9
- Gerli, E. Michael, ed., 2003. *Medieval Iberia: An Encyclopedia*. NY: Routledge. ISBN 0-415-93918-6
- Halm, Heinz. 1989. "Al-Andalus und Gothica Sors", *Der Islam*[115] 66:252–263.
- Hamilton, Michelle M., Sarah J. Portnoy, and David A. Wacks, eds. 2004. *Wine, Women, and Song: Hebrew and Arabic Literature in Medieval Iberia*. Newark, Del.: Juan de la Cuesta Hispanic Monographs.
- Harzig, Christiane, Dirk Hoerder, and Adrian Shubert. 2003. *The Historical Practice in Diversity*. Berghahn Books. ISBN 1-57181-377-2
- Jayyusi, Salma Khadra. 1992. *The Legacy of Muslim Spain*, 2 vols. Leiden–NY–Cologne: Brill [chief consultant to the editor, Manuela Marín].

- Kennedy, Hugh. 1996. *Muslim Spain and Portugal: A Political History of al-Andalus*, Longman. ISBN 0-582-49515-6
- Kraemer, Joel. 1997. "Comparing Crescent and Cross (book review)", *The Journal of Religion* 77, no. 3 (1997): 449–454.
- Kraemer, Joel. 2005. "Moses Maimonides: An Intellectual Portrait", *The Cambridge Companion to Maimonides*, ed. Kenneth Seeskin. Cambridge: Cambridge University Press. ISBN 0-521-81974-1
- Kraemer, Joel. 2008. *Maimonides: the Life and World of One of Civilization's Greatest Minds*. NY: Doubleday. ISBN 0-385-51199-X
- Lafuente y Alcántara, Emilio, trans. 1867. *Ajbar Machmua (colección de tradiciones): crónica anónima del siglo XI, dada a luz por primera vez, traducida y anotada*. Madrid: Real Academia de la Historia y Geografía. In Spanish and Arabic. Also available in the public domain online, see External Links.
- Luscombe, David and Jonathan Riley-Smith, eds. 2004. *The New Cambridge Medieval History: Volume 4, c. 1024 – c. 1198, Part 1*. Cambridge: Cambridge University Press. ISBN 0-521-41411-3
- Marcus, Ivan G., "Beyond the Sephardic mystique", *Orim*, vol. 1 (1985): 35-53.
- Marín, Manuela, ed. 1998. *The Formation of Al-Andalus*, vol. 1: *History and Society*. Aldershot: Ashgate. ISBN 0-86078-708-7
- Menocal, Maria Rosa. 2002. *Ornament of the World: How Muslims, Jews, and Christians Created a Culture of Tolerance in Medieval Spain*. Boston: Little, Brown and Company; London: Back Bay Books. ISBN 0-316-16871-8
- Monroe, James T. 1970. *Islam and the Arabs in Spanish scholarship: (Sixteenth century to the present)*. Leiden: Brill.
- Monroe, James T. 1974. *Hispano-Arabic Poetry: A Student Anthology*. Berkeley, Cal.: University of California Press.
- Netanyahu, Benzion. 1995. *The Origins Of The Inquisition in Fifteenth Century Spain*. NY: Random House ISBN 0-679-41065-1
- O'Callaghan, Joseph F. 1975. *A History of Medieval Spain*. Ithaca, NY: Cornell University Press. ISBN 0-8014-9264-5
- Omaar, Rageh. 2005. *An Islamic History of Europe*[116]. video documentary, BBC 4, August 2005.
- Reilly, Bernard F. 1993. *The Medieval Spains*. Cambridge: Cambridge University Press. ISBN 0-521-39741-3
- Roth, Norman. 1994. *Jews, Visigoths and Muslims in Medieval Spain: Cooperation and Conflict*. Leiden: Brill. ISBN 90-04-06131-2
- Sanchez-Albornoz, Claudio. 1974. *El Islam de España y el Occidente*. Madrid: Espasa-Calpe. Colección Austral; 1560. [Originally published in 1965 in the conference proceedings, *L'occidente e l'islam nell'alto*

medioevo: 2-8 aprile 1964, 2 vols. Spoleto: Centro Italiano di studi sull'Alto Medioevo. Series: Settimane di studio del Centro Italiano di studi sull'Alto Medioevo; 12. Vol. 1:149–308.]
- Schorsch, Ismar, 1989. "The myth of Sephardic supremacy", *The Leo Baeck Institute Yearbook* 34 (1989): 47–66.
- Stavans, Ilan. 2003. *The Scroll and the Cross: 1,000 Years of Jewish-Hispanic Literature*. London: Routledge. ISBN 0-415-92930-X
- *The Art of medieval Spain, A.D. 500-1200*[114]. New York: The Metropolitan Museum of Art. 1993. ISBN 0870996851.
- Wasserstein, David J. 1995. "Jewish élites in Al-Andalus", *The Jews of Medieval Islam: Community, Society and Identity*, ed. Daniel Frank. Leiden: Brill. ISBN 90-04-10404-6

External links

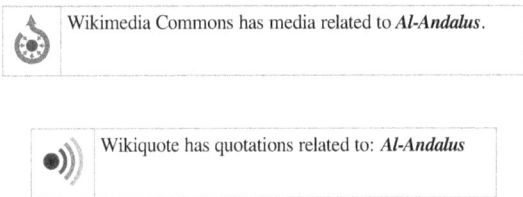

- Photocopy of the Ajbar Machmu'a, translated by Lafuente 1867[117]
- The routes of al-Andalus[118] (from the UNESCO web site)
- The Library of Iberian Resources Online[119]
- Al-Andalus Chronology and Photos[120]
- Christian Martyrs in Muslim Spain[121] by Kenneth Baxter Wolf
- The Musical Legacy of Al-Andalus[122] – historical maps, photos, and music showing the Great Mosque of Córdoba and related movements of people and culture over time
- Patricia, Countess Jellicoe, 1992, The Art of Islamic Spain[123], *Saudi Aramco World*
- "Cities of Light: The Rise and Fall of Islamic Spain"[124] (documentary film)
- Al-Andalus: the art of Islamic Spain[114], an exhibition catalog from The Metropolitan Museum of Art (fully available online as PDF)
- History of the Spanish Muslims, by [[Reinhart Dozy[125]], in French]

Coordinates: 37°N 4°W[126]

Emirate of Sicily

Emirate of Sicily	
إِمَارَةُ صِقِلِّيَة	
Province of the Aghlabid Emirate of Ifriqiya (831–909) and of the Fatimid Caliphate (909–948), after 948 autonomous emirate under the Kalbids. After 1044: various emirates in war.	
831–1091	
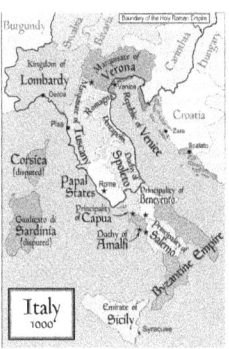 Italy in 1000. The Emirate of Sicily is coloured in light green.	
Capital	Balarme (Palermo)
Languages	Sicilian Arabic, Byzantine Greek, Vulgar Latin
Religion	Islam (state) Chalcedonian Christianity
Government	Monarchy
History	
• Established	831
• Disestablished	1091
Preceded by	Succeeded by
☧ Theme of Sicily	County of Sicily 🦁
Today part of	Italy Malta

> **Historical Arab states and dynasties**
>
> - v
> - t
> - e[127]

The **Emirate of Sicily** (Arabic: إِمَارَةُ صِقِلِّيَة) was an emirate on the island of Sicily which existed from 831 to 1091. Its capital was Palermo.

Muslim Moors, who first invaded in 652, seized control of the entire island from the Byzantine Empire in a prolonged series of conflicts from 827 to 902. An Arab-Byzantine culture developed, producing a multiconfessional and multilingual state. The Emirate was conquered by Christian Norman mercenaries under Roger I of Sicily, who founded the County of Sicily in 1071. The last Muslim city in the island, Noto, was conquered in 1091.

Sicilian Muslims remained citizens of the multi-ethnic County and subsequent Kingdom of Sicily, until those who had not already converted were expelled in the 1240s. Until the late 12th century, and probably as late as the 1220s, Muslims formed a substantial portion of the island's population. Their influence remains in some elements of the Sicilian language, as well as surnames and locations.

First Muslim attempts to conquer Sicily

In 535, Emperor Justinian I returned Sicily to the Roman Empire, now ruled from Constantinople exclusively. As the power of what is now known as the Byzantine Empire waned in the West, Sicily was invaded by the Rashidun Caliphate during the reign of Caliph Uthman in the year 652. However, this first invasion was short-lived, and the Muslims left soon after. By the end of the 7th century, with the Umayyad conquest of North Africa, the Muslims had captured the nearby port city of Carthage, allowing them to build shipyards and a permanent base from which to launch more sustained attacks.

Around 700, the island of Pantelleria was captured by Muslims, and it was only discord among the Muslims that prevented an attempted invasion of Sicily coming next. Instead, trading agreements were arranged with the Byzantines, and Muslims merchants were allowed to trade goods at the Sicilian ports.

The first true conquest expedition was launched in 740; in that year the Muslim prince Habib, who had participated on the 728 attack, successfully captured Syracuse. Ready to conquer the whole island, they were however forced to return to Tunisia by a Berber revolt. A second attack in 752 aimed only to sack the same city.

Revolt of Euphemius and gradual Muslim conquest of the island

In 826 Euphemius, the commander of the Byzantine fleet of Sicily, forced a nun to marry him. Emperor Michael II caught wind of the matter and ordered that General Constantine end the marriage and cut off Euphemius' nose. Euphemius rose up, killed Constantine and then occupied Syracuse; he in turn was defeated and driven out to North Africa. He offered rule of Sicily over to Ziyadat Allah the Aghlabid Emir of Tunisia in return for a place as a general and safety; a Muslim army was sent.

The latter agreed to conquer Sicily, promising to give it to Euphemius in exchange for a yearly tribute, and entrusted its conquest to the 70-year-old qadi Asad ibn al-Furat. The Muslim force counted 10,000 infantry, 700 cavalry and 100 ships, reinforced by Euphemius' ships and, after the landing at Mazara del Vallo. A first battle against the loyal Byzantine troops occurred on July 15, 827, near Mazara, resulting in an Aghlabid victory.

Asad subsequently conquered the southern shore of the island and laid siege to Syracuse. After a year of siege, and an attempted mutiny, his troops were however able to defeat a large army sent from Palermo, also backed by a Venetian fleet led by Doge Giustiniano Participazio. But when a plague killed many of the Muslim troops, as well as Asad himself, the Muslims retreated to the castle of Mineo. Later they returned to the offensive, but failed to conquer Castrogiovanni (the modern Enna, where Euphemius died) and retreated back to Mazara.

In 830 they received a strong reinforcement of 30,000 Ifriqiyan and Andalusian troops. The Iberian Muslims defeated the Byzantine commander Teodotus in July–August of that year, but again a plague forced them to return to Mazara

Figure 48: *Arab-Norman art and architecture combined Occidental features (such as the Classical pillars and friezes) with typical Arabic decorations and calligraphy.*

and then to Ifriqiya. The Ifriqiyan units sent to besiege Palermo managed to capture it after a year long siege in September 831.[128] Palermo became the Muslim capital of Sicily, renamed al-Madinah ("The City").[129]

The conquest was a see-saw affair; with considerable resistance and many internal struggles, it took over a century for Byzantine Sicily to be conquered. Syracuse held out for a long time but fell in 878, Taormina fell in 902, and the last Byzantine outpost was taken in 965.

Period as an emirate

In succession, Sicily was ruled by the Sunni Aghlabid dynasty in Tunisia and the Shiite Fatimids in Egypt. However, throughout this period, Sunni Muslims formed the majority of the Muslim community in Sicily, with most (if not all) of the people of Palermo being Sunni, leading to their hostility to the Shia Kalbids. The Sunni population of the island was replenished following sectarian rebellions across north Africa from 943 to 47 against the Fatimids harsh religious policies, leading to several waves of refugees fleeing to Sicily in an attempt to escape Fatimid retaliation. The Byzantines took advantage of temporary discord to occupy the eastern end of the island for several years.

Figure 49: *Arab musicians in Palermo*

After suppressing a revolt the Fatimid caliph Ismail al-Mansur appointed al-Hasan al-Kalbi (948–964) as Emir of Sicily. He successfully managed to control the continuously revolting Byzantines and founded the Kalbid dynasty. Raids into Southern Italy continued under the Kalbids into the 11th century, and in 982 a German army under Otto II, Holy Roman Emperor was defeated near Crotone in Calabria. With Emir Yusuf al-Kalbi (986–998) a period of steady decline began. Under al-Akhal (1017–1037) the dynastic conflict intensified, with factions within the ruling family allying themselves variously with the Byzantine Empire and the Zirids. After this period, Al-Mu'izz ibn Badis attempted to annex the island for the Zirids, while intervening in the affairs of the feuding Muslims; however, the attempt ultimately failed.

Sicily under Arab rule

The new Arab rulers initiated land reforms, which in turn increased productivity and encouraged the growth of smallholdings, a dent to the dominance of the landed estates. The Arabs further improved irrigation systems through Qanats. Introducing oranges, lemons, pistachio and sugarcane to Sicily. A description of Palermo was given by Ibn Hawqal, a Baghdad merchant who visited Sicily in 950. A walled suburb called the Kasr (the palace) is the center of Palermo

Figure 50: *Aghlabid quarter dinar minted in Sicily, 879*

until today, with the great Friday mosque on the site of the later Roman cathedral. The suburb of Al-Khalisa (Kalsa) contained the Sultan's palace, baths, a mosque, government offices, and a private prison. Ibn Hawqual reckoned 7,000 individual butchers trading in 150 shops. By 1050, Palermo had a population of 350,000, making it one of the largest cities in Europe, but behind Islamic Spain's capital Córdoba and the Byzantine capital of Constantinople, which had populations over 450-500,000. Palermo's population dropped to 150,000 under Norman rule, while there was a greater decline in Córdoba's population as Muslims there weakened; by 1330 Palermo's population had declined to 51,000.

Arab traveler, geographer, and poet Ibn Jubair visited the area in the end of the 12th century and described Al-Kasr and Al-Khalisa (Kalsa):

> *The capital is endowed with two gifts, splendor and wealth. It contains all the real and imagined beauty that anyone could wish. Splendor and grace adorn the piazzas and the countryside; the streets and highways are wide, and the eye is dazzled by the beauty of its situation. It is a city full of marvels, with buildings similar to those of Córdoba [sic], built of limestone. A permanent stream of water from four springs runs through the city. There are so many mosques that they are impossible to count. Most of them also serve as schools. The eye is dazzled by all this splendor.*

Throughout this reign, continued revolts by Byzantine Sicilians occurred, especially in the east, and part of the lands were even re-occupied before being quashed.

The local population conquered by the Muslims were Romanized Catholic Sicilians in Western Sicily and Greek speaking Christians mainly in the eastern

Figure 51: *Roger I of Sicily receiving the keys of Palermo*

half of the island, but there were also a significant number of Jews.[130] Christians and Jews were tolerated under Muslim rule as dhimmis, but were subject to some restrictions. The dhimmis were also required to pay the jizya, or poll tax, and the kharaj or land tax, but were exempt from the tax that Muslims had to pay (Zakaat). Under Arab rule there were different categories of Jizya payers, but their common denominator was the payment of the Jizya as a mark of subjection to Muslim rule in exchange for protection against foreign and internal aggression. The conquered population could avoid this subservient status by converting to Islam. Whether by honest religious conviction or compulsion large numbers of native Sicilians converted to Islam. However, even after 100 years of Islamic rule, numerous Greek speaking Christian communities prospered, especially in north-eastern Sicily, as dhimmis. This was largely a result of the Jizya system which allowed co-existence. This co-existence with the conquered population fell apart after the reconquest of Sicily, particularly following the death of King William II of Sicily in 1189.

Decline and "Taifa" period

The Emirate of Sicily began to fragment as intra-dynastic quarrels took place within the Muslim regime. In 1044, under emir Hasan al-Samsam, who established al-Samsam Emirate of Sicily, the island fragmented into four qadits, or small fiefdoms: the qadit of Trapani, Marsala, Mazara and Sciacca, a certain Abdallah ibn Mankut; that of Girgenti, Castrogiovanni and Castronuovo (Ibn al-Hawwàs); that of Palermo and Catania; and that of Syracuse (Ibn Thumna). By 1065, all of them had been unified by Ayyub ibn Tamim, the son of the Zirid emir of Ifriqiyya. In 1068 he left Sicily, and what remained under Muslim control fell under two qadits: one, led by Ibn Abbad (known as Benavert in western chronicles) in Syracuse, and the other under Hammud in Qas'r Ianni (modern Enna).

By the 11th century mainland southern Italian powers were hiring Norman mercenaries, who were Christian descendants of the Vikings; it was the Normans under Roger I who captured Sicily from the Muslims. The Norman Robert Guiscard, son of Tancred, invaded Sicily in 1060 after taking Apulia and Calabria, Roger I occupied Messina with an army of 700 knights. The Zirids of North Africa sent a support force, led by Ali and Ayyub ibn Tamin. However, Sicilians and Africans were defeated in 1063, in the Battle of Cerami. The sizeable Christian population rose up against the ruling Muslims.[131] In 1068, Roger de Hauteville and his men defeated again the Muslims forces commanded by Ayu ibn Tamim in Misilmeri. The Africans left Sicily in disarray after the defeat and Catania fell to the Normans in 1071, followed, after one year of siege, by Palermo in 1072. Trapani capitulated the same year.

The loss of the main port cities dealt a severe blow to Muslim power on the island. The last pocket of active resistance was Syracuse governed by Ibn Abbad (known by the Normans as Benavert). He defeated Jordan, son of Roger of Sicily in 1075, and occupied Catania again in 1081 and raided Calabria shortly after. However, Roger besieged Syracuse in 1086, and Ibn Abbad tried to break the siege with naval battle, in which he died accidentally. Syracuse surrendered after this defeat. His wife and son fled to Noto and Butera. Meanwhile the city of Qas'r Ianni (Enna) was still ruled by its emir, Ibn Al-Hawas, who held out for years. His successor, Hamud, surrendered, and converted to Christianity, only in 1087. After his conversion, Ibn Hamud subsequently became part of the Christian nobility and retired with his family to an estate in Calabria provided by Roger I. In 1091, Butera and Noto in the southern tip of Sicily and the island of Malta, the last Arab strongholds, fell to the Christians with ease. After the conquest of Sicily, the Normans removed the local emir, Yusuf Ibn Abdallah from power, but did so by respecting Arab customs.

Aftermath

The Norman Kingdom of Sicily under Roger II has been characterized as multi-ethnic in nature and religiously tolerant.[132] Normans, Jews, Muslim

Figure 52: *A 12th century Arab-Norman painting depicting Roger II*

Arabs, Byzantine Greeks, Lombards and native Sicilians lived in relative harmony.[133,134] Arabic remained a language of government and administration for at least a century into Norman rule, and traces remain in the language of Sicily and evidently more in the language of Malta today. The Muslims also maintained their domination of industry, retailing and production, while Muslim artisans and expert knowledge in government and administration were highly sought after.

However, after the Normans had conquered the island Muslims were faced with the choice of voluntary departure or subjection to Christian rule. Many Muslims chose to leave, provided they had the means to do so. "The transformation of Sicily into a Christian island", remarks Abulafia, "was also, paradoxically, the work of those whose culture was under threat".[135,136] Despite the presence of an Arab-speaking Christian population, it was Greek churchmen who attracted Muslim peasants to receive baptism and even adopt Greek Christian names; in several instances, Christian serfs with Greek names listed in the Monreale registers had living Muslim parents.[137,138] The Norman rulers followed a policy of steady Latinization by bringing in thousands of Italian settlers from the northwest and south of Italy, and some others from southeast France. To this day there are communities in central Sicily which speak the Gallo-Italic dialect. Some Muslims chose to feign conversion, but such a remedy could only provide individual protection and could not sustain a community.[139]

"Lombard" pogroms against Muslims started in the 1160s. Muslim and Christian communities in Sicily became increasingly geographically separated. The island's Muslim communities were mainly isolated beyond an internal frontier which divided the south-western half of the island from the Christian north-east. Sicilian Muslims, a subject population, were dependent on the mercy of their Christian masters and, ultimately, on royal protection. When King William the Good died in 1189, this royal protection was lifted, and the door was opened for widespread attacks against the island's Muslims. This destroyed any lingering hope of coexistence, however unequal the respective populations might have been. Henry VI's death in 1197, and that of his wife Constance a year later, plunged Sicily into political turmoil. With the loss of royal protection and with Frederick II still an infant in papal custody, Sicily became a battleground for rival German and papal forces. The island's Muslim rebels sided with German warlords like Markward von Anweiler. In response, Innocent III declared a crusade against Markward, alleging that he had made an unholy alliance with the Saracens of Sicily. Nevertheless, in 1206 that same pope attempted to convince the Muslim leaders to remain loyal.[140] By this time, the Muslim rebellion was critical, with Muslims in control of Jato, Entella, Platani, Celso, Calatrasi, Corleone (taken in 1208), Guastanella and Cinisi. In other words, the Muslim revolt extended throughout a whole stretch of western Sicily. The rebels were led by Muhammad Ibn Abbād. He called himself the "prince of believers", struck his own coins, and attempted to find Muslim support from other parts of the Muslim world.[141]

However, Frederick II, no longer a child, responded by launching a series of campaigns against the Muslim rebels in 1221. The Hohenstaufen forces rooted out the defenders of Jato, Entella, and the other fortresses. Rather than exterminate the Muslims, in 1223, Frederick II and the Christians began the first deportations of Muslims to Lucera in Apulia.[142] A year later, expeditions were sent against Malta and Djerba, to establish royal control and prevent their Muslim populations from helping the rebels. Paradoxically, Saracen archers were a common component of these "Christian" armies from this era.[143]

The House of Hohenstaufen and their successors (Capetian House of Anjou and Aragonese House of Barcelona) gradually "Latinized" Sicily over the course of two centuries, and this social process laid the groundwork for the introduction of Latin (as opposed to Byzantine) Catholicism. The process of Latinization was fostered largely by the Roman Church and its liturgy. The annihilation of Islam in Sicily was completed by the late 1240s, when the final deportations to Lucera took place.

List of emirs

- al-Hasan ibn Ali al-Kalbi (948–953)
- Ahmad ibn al-Hasan al-Muizziyya (953–969)
- Yaish (usurper, 969)
- Ahmad ibn al-Hasan al-Muizziyya (969–970)
- Abu'l-Qasim Ali ibn al-Hasan al-Kalbi (970–982)
- Jabir ibn 'Ali (982–983)
- Ja'far ibn Muhammad (983–986)
- Abd Allah ibn Muhammad (986)
- Yusuf al-Kalbi (986–998)
- Ja'far OO (998–1019)
- Ahmad II al-Akhal (1017–1037)
- Abd Allah Abu Hafs (1035–1040, usurper; defeated and killed Ahmad II in 1037)
- Hasan al-Samsam (1040–1044; died 1053)

Taifa period

- Catania :(1053 - ?), Ibn al-Maklatí, defeated by Ibn Thumna
- Syracuse and later Catania (1053 - 1062) : Muhammed ibn Ibrahim (Ibn Thumna)
- Agrigento and Castrogiovanni (1053 - 1065) : Alí ibn Nima (Ibn al-Hawwàs)
- Trapani and Mazara (1053 - 1071) : Abdallah ibn Mankut
- Ayyub ibn Tamim (Zirid) : (1065-1068) (united the taifas)[144]
- Palermo (1068-1071) : republica
- Agrigento and Castrogiovanni(1065- 1087) :Hammad
- Syracuse and Catania :(1071- 1086) : Ibn Abbad (Benavert)

Sources

- Previte-Orton, C. W. (1971). *The Shorter Cambridge Medieval History*. Cambridge: Cambridge University Press.

External links

- Sicily(Italy):A Great Centre of the Islamic Civilization[145]

Islamic world contributions to Medieval Europe

During the high medieval period, the Islamic world was at its cultural peak, supplying information and ideas to Europe, via Andalusia, Sicily and the Crusader kingdoms in the Levant. These included Latin translations of the Greek Classics and of Arabic texts in astronomy, mathematics, science, and medicine. Other contributions included technological and scientific innovations via the Silk Road, including Chinese inventions such as paper and gunpowder.

The Islamic world also influenced other aspects of medieval European culture, partly by original innovations made during the Islamic Golden Age, including various fields such as the arts, agriculture, alchemy, music, pottery, etc.

Many Arabic loanwords in Western European languages, including English, mostly via Old French, date from this period.[147] This includes traditional star names such as Aldebaran, scientific terms like *alchemy* (whence also *chemistry*), *algebra*, *algorithm*, etc. and names of commodities such as *sugar*, *camphor*, *cotton*, etc.

Transmission routes

Europe and the Islamic lands had multiple points of contact during the Middle Ages. The main points of transmission of Islamic knowledge to Europe lay in Sicily and in Spain, particularly in Toledo (with Gerard of Cremone, 1114–1187, following the conquest of the city by Spanish Christians in 1085). In Sicily, following the Islamic conquest of the island in 965 and its reconquest by the Normans in 1091, a syncretistic Norman-Arab-Byzantine culture developed, exemplified by rulers such as King Roger II, who had Islamic soldiers, poets and scientists at his court. The Moroccan Muhammad al-Idrisi wrote *The Book of Pleasant Journeys into Faraway Lands* or *Tabula Rogeriana*, one of the greatest geographical treatises of the Middle Ages, for Roger.[148]

The Crusades also intensified exchanges between Europe and the Levant, with the Italian maritime republics taking a major role in these exchanges. In the Levant, in such cities as Antioch, Arab and Latin cultures intermixed intensively.[149]

During the 11th and 12th centuries, many Christian scholars travelled to Muslim lands to learn sciences. Notable examples include Leonardo Fibonacci (c. 1170 –c. 1250), Adelard of Bath (c. 1080–c. 1152) and Constantine the

Islamic world contributions to Medieval Europe 77

Figure 53: *A Christian and a Muslim playing chess, illustration from the Book of Games of Alfonso X (c. 1285).*[146]

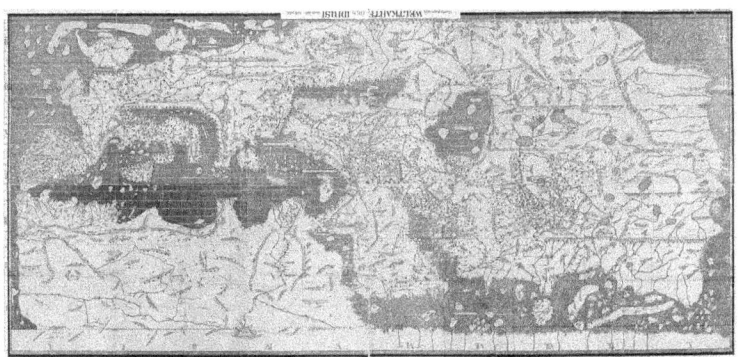

Figure 54: *The Tabula Rogeriana, drawn by Al-Idrisi for Roger II of Sicily in 1154, was one of the most advanced world maps of its era.*

Figure 55: *An medieval Arabic representation of Aristotle teaching a student.*

African (1017–1087). From the 11th to the 14th centuries, numerous European students attended Muslim centers of higher learning (which the author calls "universities") to study medicine, philosophy, mathematics, cosmography and other subjects.

Aristotelianism and other philosophies

In the Middle East, many classical Greek texts, especially the works of Aristotle, were translated into Syriac during the 6th and 7th centuries by Nestorian, Melkite or Jacobite monks living in Palestine, or by Greek exiles from Athens or Edessa who visited Islamic centres of higher learning. The Islamic world then kept, translated, and developed many of these texts, especially in centers of learning such as Baghdad, where a "House of Wisdom" with thousands of manuscripts existed as early as 832. These texts were in turn translated into Latin by scholars such as Michael Scot (who made translations of *Historia Animalium* and *On the Soul* as well as of Averroes's commentaries) during the Middle Ages. Eastern Christians played an important role in exploiting this knowledge, especially through the Christian Aristotelian School of Baghdad in the 11th and 12th centuries.

Later Latin translations of these texts originated in multiple places. Toledo, Spain (with Gerard of Cremona's *Almagest*) and Sicily became the main points

Figure 56: *Averroes was influential in the rise of secular thought in Western Europe.*

of transmission of knowledge from the Islamic world to Europe. Burgundio of Pisa (died 1193) discovered lost texts of Aristotle in Antioch and translated them into Latin.

From Islamic Spain, the Arabic philosophical literature was translated into Hebrew, Latin, and Ladino. The Jewish philosopher Moses Maimonides, Muslim sociologist-historian Ibn Khaldun, Carthage citizen Constantine the African who translated Greek medical texts, and Al-Khwarizmi's collation of mathematical techniques were important figures of the Golden Age.

Avicennism and Averroism are terms for the revival of the Peripatetic school in medieval Europe due to the influence of Avicenna and Averroes, respectively. Avicenna was an important commentator on the works of Aristotle, modifying it with his own original thinking in some areas, notably logic.[150] The main significance of Latin Avicennism lies in the interpretation of Avicennian doctrines such as the nature of the soul and his existence-essence distinction, along with the debates and censure that they raised in scholastic Europe. This was particularly the case in Paris, where so-called Arabic culture was proscribed in 1210, though the influence of his psychology and theory of knowledge upon William of Auvergne and Albertus Magnus have been noted.

Figure 57: *Imaginary debate between Averroes and Porphyry. Monfredo de Monte Imperiali Liber de herbis, 14th century.*[153]

The effects of Avicennism in were later submerged by the much more influential Averroism, the Aristotelianism of Averroes, one of the most influential Muslim philosophers in the West.[151] Averroes disagreed with Avicenna's interpretations of Aristotle in areas such as the unity of the intellect, and it was his interpretation of Aristotle which had the most influence in medieval Europe. Dante Aligheri argues along Averroist lines for a secularist theory of the state in *De Monarchia*.[152] Averroes also developed the concept of "existence precedes essence".

Al-Ghazali also had an important influence on medieval Christian philosopher along with Jewish thinkers like Maimonides.[154]

George Makdisi (1989) has suggested that two particular aspects of Renaissance humanism have their roots in the medieval Islamic world, the "art of *dictation*, called in Latin, *ars dictaminis*," and "the humanist attitude toward classical language". He notes that dictation was a necessary part of Arabic scholarship (where the vowel sounds need to be added correctly based on the spoken word), and argues that the medieval Italian use of the term "ars dictaminis" makes best sense in this context. He also believes that the medieval humanist favouring of classical Latin over medieval Latin makes most sense in the context of a reaction to Arabic scholarship, with its study of the classical Arabic of the Koran in preference to medieval Arabic.

Sciences

A page from Frederick Rosen's 1831 edition of Al-Khwarizmi's *Algebra* alongside the corresponding English translation.

During the Islamic Golden Age, certain advances were made in scientific fields, notably in mathematics and astronomy (algebra, spherical trigonometry), and in chemistry, etc. which were later also transmitted to the West.[155]

Stefan of Pise translated into Latin around 1127 an Arab manual of medical theory. The method of algorism for performing arithmetic with Indian-Arabic numerals was developed by the Persian al-Khwarizmi in the 9th century, and introduced in Europe by Leonardo Fibonacci (1170–1250).[156] A translation by Robert of Chester of the *Algebra* by al-Kharizmi is known as early as 1145. Ibn al-Haytham (Alhazen, 980–1037) compiled treatises on optical sciences, which were used as references by Newton and Descartes. Medical sciences were also highly developed in Islam as testified by the Crusaders, who relied on Arab doctors on numerous occasions. Joinville reports he was saved in 1250 by a "Saracen" doctor.[157]

Contributing to the growth of European science was the major search by European scholars such as Gerard of Cremona for new learning. These scholars were interested in ancient Greek philosophical and scientific texts (notably the *Almagest*) which were not obtainable in Latin in Western Europe, but which had survived and been translated into Arabic in the Muslim world. Gerard was said to have made his way to Toledo in Spain and learnt Arabic specifically because of his "love of the *Almagest*". While there he took advantage of the "abundance of books in Arabic on every subject".[158] Islamic

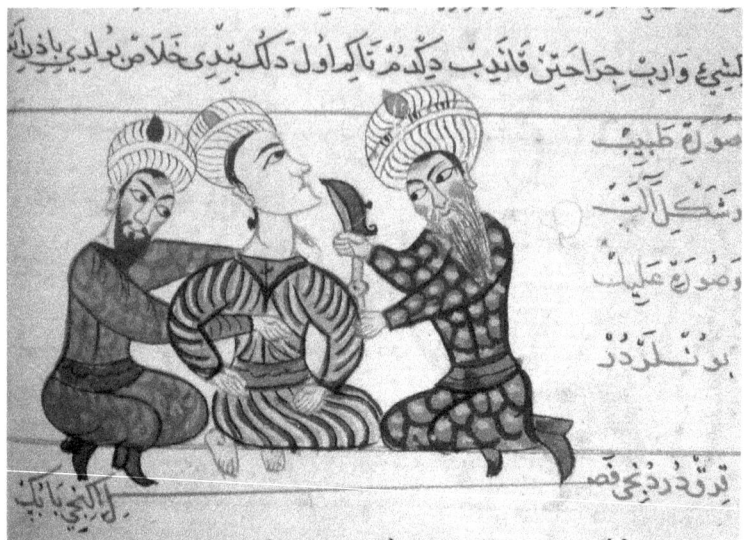

Figure 58: *Surgical operation, 15th-century Turkish manuscript*

Spain and Sicily were particularly productive areas because of the proximity of multi-lingual scholars. These scholars translated many scientific and philosophical texts from Arabic into Latin.[159,160] Gerard personally translated 87 books from Arabic into Latin, including the *Almagest*, and also Muhammad ibn Mūsā al-Khwārizmī's *On Algebra and Almucabala*, Jabir ibn Aflah's *Elementa astronomica*, al-Kindi's *On Optics*, Ahmad ibn Muhammad ibn Kathīr al-Farghānī's *On Elements of Astronomy on the Celestial Motions*, al-Farabi's *On the Classification of the Sciences*,[161] the chemical and medical works of Rhazes, the works of Thabit ibn Qurra and Hunayn ibn Ishaq,[162] and the works of Arzachel, Jabir ibn Aflah, the Banū Mūsā, Abū Kāmil Shujā ibn Aslam, Abu al-Qasim al-Zahrawi (Abulcasis), and Ibn al-Haytham (including the *Book of Optics*).

Alchemy

Western alchemy was directly dependent upon Arabic sources. The Latin alchemical works of "Geber" (Jābir ibn Hayyān) were standard texts for European alchemists. The exact attribution of these works remains a matter of some controversy. Some are undoubtedly translations from Arabic from works attributed to Jābir ibn Hayyān, including the *Kitab al-Kimya* (titled *Book of the Composition of Alchemy* in Europe), translated by Robert of Chester (1144);[163] and the *Book of Seventy*, translated by Gerard of Cremona (before 1187).[164]

Figure 59: *Geber depicted in Liebig's Extract of Meat Company trading card "Chimistes Celebres", 1929.*

Whether these were actually written by one man (or whether indeed Jābir was a real historical figure) is disputed, but there is no doubting the influence on medieval European alchemy of the translated Arabic works.[165]</ref> The alchemical works of Muhammad ibn Zakarīya Rāzi (Rhazes) were translated into Latin around the 12th century. Several technical Arabic words from Arabic alchemical works, such as *alkali*, found their way into European languages and became part of scientific vocabulary.

Astronomy, mathematics, physics

The translation of Al-Khwarizmi's work greatly influenced mathematics in Europe. As Professor Victor J. Katz writes: "Most early algebra works in Europe in fact recognized that the first algebra works in that continent were translations of the work of al-Khwärizmï and other Islamic authors. There was also some awareness that much of plane and spherical trigonometry could be attributed to Islamic authors". The words algorithm, deriving from Al-Khwarizmi's Latinized name Algorismi, and algebra, deriving from the title of his AD 820 book *Hisab al-jabr w'al-muqabala, Kitab al-Jabr wa-l-Muqabala* are themselves Arabic loanwords. This and other Arabic astronomical and mathematical works, such as those by al-Battani and Muhammad al-Fazari's *Great Sindhind* (based on the *Surya Siddhanta* and the works of Brahmagupta).[166] were translated into Latin during the 12th century.

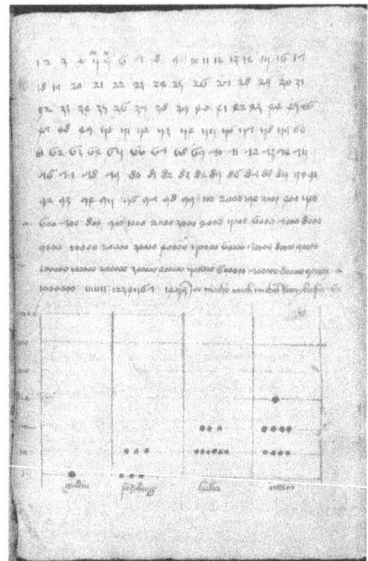

Figure 60: *A German manuscript page teaching use of Arabic numerals (Hans Talhoffer, 1459)*

Figure 61: *A European and an Arab practicing geometry together. 15th-century manuscript*

Figure 62: *Astrolabe quadrant, England, 1388*

Al-Khazini's *Zij as-Sanjari* (1115–1116) was translated into Greek by Gregory Choniades in the 13th century and was studied in the Byzantine Empire.[167] The astronomical modifications to the Ptolemaic model made by al-Battani and Averroes led to non-Ptolemaic models produced by Mo'ayyeduddin Urdi (Urdi lemma), Nasīr al-Dīn al-Tūsī (Tusi-couple) and Ibn al-Shatir, which were later adapted into the Copernican heliocentric model. Abū al-Rayhān al-Bīrūnī's *Ta'rikh al-Hind* and *Kitab al-qanun al-Mas'udi* were translated into Latin as *Indica* and *Canon Mas'udicus* respectively.

Fibonacci presented the first complete European account of Arabic numerals and the Hindu-Arabic numeral system in his *Liber Abaci* (1202).

Al-Jayyani's *The book of unknown arcs of a sphere* (a treatise on spherical trigonometry) had a "strong influence on European mathematics". Regiomantus' *On Triangles* (c. 1463) certainly took his material on spherical trigonometry (without acknowledgement) from Arab sources. Much of the material was taken from the 12th-century work of Jabir ibn Aflah, as noted in the 16th century by Gerolamo Cardano.[168]

A short verse used by Fulbert of Chartres (952-970 –1028) to help remember some of the brightest stars in the sky gives us the earliest known use of Arabic loanwords in a Latin text: "Aldebaran stands out in Taurus, Menke and Rigel in Gemini, and Frons and bright Calbalazet in Leo. Scorpio, you have Galbalagrab; and you, Capricorn, Deneb. You, Batanalhaut, are alone enough for Pisces."

Ibn al-Haytham (Alhazen) wrote the *Book of Optics* (1021), in which he developed a theory of vision and light which built on the work of the Roman writer Ptolemy (but which rejected Ptolemy's theory that light was emitted by the eye, insisting instead that light rays entered the eye), and was the most significant advance in this field until Kepler. The *Book of Optics* was an important stepping stone in the history of the scientific method and history of optics.[169] The Latin translation of the *Book of Optics* influenced the works of many later European scientists, including Roger Bacon and Johannes Kepler.[170] The book also influenced other aspects of European culture. In religion, for example, John Wycliffe, the intellectual progenitor of the Protestant Reformation, referred to Alhazen in discussing the seven deadly sins in terms of the distortions in the seven types of mirrors analyzed in *De aspectibus*. In literature, Alhazen's *Book of Optics* is praised in Guillaume de Lorris' *Roman de la Rose*. In art, the *Book of Optics* laid the foundations for the linear perspective technique and may have influenced the use of optical aids in Renaissance art (see Hockney-Falco thesis). These same techniques were later employed in the maps made by European cartographers such as Paolo Toscanelli during the Age of Exploration.

The theory of motion developed by Avicenna from Aristotelian physics may have influenced Jean Buridan's theory of impetus (the ancestor of the inertia and momentum concepts). The work of Galileo Galilei on classical mechanics (superseding Aristotelian physics) was also influenced by earlier medieval physics writers, including Avempace.[171]

The magnetic compass, a Chinese invention, is first mentioned in Arabic sources of c. 1300, by the Yemeni Sultan al-Ashraf and by Egyptian astronomer Ibn Sim'un.

Other notable works include those of Nur Ed-Din Al Betrugi, notably *On the Motions of the Heavens*, Abu Mashar's *Introduction to Astrology*,[172] Abū Kāmil Shujā ibn Aslam's *Algebra*,[173] and *De Proprietatibus Elementorum*, an Arabic work on geology written by a pseudo-Aristotle. B

Medicine

One of the most important medical works to be translated was Avicenna's *The Canon of Medicine* (1025), which was translated into Latin and then disseminated in manuscript and printed form throughout Europe. It remained a standard medical textbook in Europe until the early modern period, and during the 15th and 16th centuries alone, *The Canon of Medicine* was published

Figure 63: *European depiction of the Persian doctor al-Razi, in Gerard of Cremona's Receuil des traités de médecine (1250–1260). Gerard de Cremona translated numerous works by Muslim scholars, such as al-Razi and Ibn Sina.*[174]

Figure 64: *Syrian medicinal jars c. 1300, excavated in Fenchurch Street, London. London Museum*

Figure 65: *Facade of a meeting between a Muslim scholar and a Frankish lord*

more than thirty-five times.[175] Avicenna noted the contagious nature of some infectious diseases (which he attributed to "traces" left in the air by a sick person), and discussed how to effectively test new medicines.[176] He also wrote *The Book of Healing*, a more general encyclopedia of science and philosophy, which became another popular textbook in Europe. Muhammad ibn Zakarīya Rāzi) wrote the *Comprehensive Book of Medicine*, with its careful description of and distinction between measles and smallpox, which was also influential in Europe. Abu al-Qasim al-Zahrawi wrote *Kitab al-Tasrif*, an encyclopedia of medicine which was particularly famed for its section on surgery. It included descriptions and diagrams of over 200 surgical instruments, many of which he developed. The surgery section was translated into Latin by Gerard of Cremona in the 12th century, and used in European medical schools for centuries, still being reprinted in the 1770s.[177,178]

Other medical Arabic works translated into Latin during the medieval period include the works of Razi and Avicenna (including *The Book of Healing* and *The Canon of Medicine*),[179] and Ali ibn Abbas al-Majusi's medical encyclopedia, *The Complete Book of the Medical Art*. Mark of Toledo in the early 13th century translated the Qur'an as well as various medical works.[180]

Figure 66: *19th-century depiction of La Zisa, Palermo, showing Arab-Norman art and architecture combining Occidental features (such as the Classical pillars and friezes) with Islamic decorations and calligraphy.*[181]

Technology and culture

Agriculture and textiles

Various fruits and vegetables were introduced to Europe in this period via the Middle East and North Africa, some from as far as China and India, including the artichoke, spinach, and aubergine.[182]

Arts

Islamic decorative arts were highly valued imports to Europe throughout the Middle Ages. Largely because of accidents of survival, most surviving examples are those that were in the possession of the church. In the early period textiles were especially important, used for church vestments, shrouds, hangings and clothing for the elite. Islamic pottery of everyday quality was still preferred to European wares. Because decoration was mostly ornamental, or small hunting scenes and the like, and inscriptions were not understood, Islamic objects did not offend Christian sensibilities.[183] Medieval art in Sicily is interesting stylistically because of the mixture of Norman, Arab and Byzantine influences in areas such as mosaics and metal inlays, sculpture, and bronze-working.

Figure 67: *Pseudo-Kufic script in the Virgin Mary's halo, detail of Adoration of the Magi (1423) by Gentile da Fabriano. The script is further divided by rosettes like those on Mamluk dishes.*[184]

Writing

The Arabic Kufic script was often imitated for decorative effect in the West during the Middle Ages and the Renaissance, to produce what is known as pseudo-Kufic: "Imitations of Arabic in European art are often described as pseudo-Kufic, borrowing the term for an Arabic script that emphasizes straight and angular strokes, and is most commonly used in Islamic architectural decoration".[185] Numerous cases of pseudo-Kufic are known from European art from around the 10th to the 15th century; usually the characters are meaningless, though sometimes a text has been copied. Pseudo-Kufic would be used as writing or as decorative elements in textiles, religious halos or frames. Many are visible in the paintings of Giotto. The exact reason for the incorporation of pseudo-Kufic in early Renaissance painting is unclear. It seems that Westerners mistakenly associated 13th- and 14th-century Middle-Eastern scripts as being identical with the scripts current during Jesus's time, and thus found natural to represent early Christians in association with them:[186] *"In Renaissance art, pseudo-Kufic script was used to decorate the costumes of Old Testament heroes like David"*. Another reason might be that artist wished to express a cultural universality for the Christian faith, by blending together various written languages, at a time when the church had strong international ambitions.[187]

Figure 68: *The Somerset House Conference (1604) artist unknown, shows English and Spanish diplomats gathered around a table covered by an Oriental carpet.*

Carpets

Carpets of Middle-Eastern origin, either from the Ottoman Empire, the Levant or the Mamluk state of Egypt or Northern Africa, were a significant sign of wealth and luxury in Europe, as demonstrated by their frequent occurrence as important decorative features in paintings from the 13th century and continuing into the Baroque period. Such carpets, together with Pseudo-Kufic script offer an interesting example of the integration of Eastern elements into European painting, most particularly those depicting religious subjects.

Music

A number of musical instruments used in European music were influenced by Arabic musical instruments, including the rebec (ancestor of the violin) from the *rebab*, the guitar from *qitara*, the naker from *naqareh* and the shawm and dulzaina from the reed instruments *zamr* and *al-zurna*.

There are many different theories regarding the origins of the troubadour tradition; one of the most commonly held theories is that it had Arabic origins. William of Aquitaine, the first troubadour whose work survives, had extensive contact with the Islamic world in the Crusade of 1101 and in the Reconquista in Spain (where he was given a rock crystal vase by a Muslim ally). In his

Figure 69: *Muslim and Christian playing lutes. Miniature from Cantigas de Santa Maria by King Alfonso X*

study, Lévi-Provençal is said to have found four Arabo-Hispanic verses nearly or completely recopied in William's manuscript. According to historic sources, William VIII, the father of William IX, brought to Poitiers hundreds of Muslim prisoners.[188] The hypothesis that the troubadour tradition was created, more or less, by William after his experience of Moorish arts while fighting with the Reconquista in Spain was championed by Ramón Menéndez Pidal in the early 20th century, but its origins go back as far as Giammaria Barbieri in the 16th century. Certainly "a body of song of comparable intensity, profanity and eroticism [existed] in Arabic from the second half of the 9th century onwards."[189]

Technology

A number of technologies in the Islamic world were adopted in European medieval technology. These included various crops; various astronomical instruments, including the Greek astrolabe which Arab astronomers developed and refined into such instruments as the *Quadrans Vetus*, a universal horary quadrant which could be used for any latitude,[190] and the *Saphaea*, a universal astrolabe invented by Abū Ishāq Ibrāhīm al-Zarqālī;[191] the astronomical sextant; various surgical instruments, including refinements on older forms and completely new inventions; and advanced gearing in waterclocks and automata.[192]

Islamic world contributions to Medieval Europe 93

Figure 70: *Syrian or Egyptian pieces of glass with Arabic inscriptions, excavated in London. London Museum.*

Figure 71: *Early-16th century Andalusian dish with pseudo-Arabic script around the edge, excavated in London. London Museum.*

Figure 72: *The Aldrevandini Beaker, Venetian glass with enamel decoration derived from Islamic technique and style. c. 1330.*

Distillation was known to the Greeks and Romans, but was rediscovered in medieval Europe through the Arabs. The word alcohol (to describe the liquid produced by distillation) comes from Arabic *al-kuhl*. The word alembic (via the Greek Ambix) comes from Arabic *al-anbiq*. Islamic examples of complex water clocks and automata are believed to have strongly influenced the European craftsmen who produced the first mechanical clocks in the 13th century.[193]

The importation of both the ancient and new technology from the Middle East and the Orient to Renaissance Europe represented "one of the largest technology transfers in world history."

In an influential 1974 paper, historian Andrew Watson suggested that there had been an Arab Agricultural Revolution between 700 and 1100, which had diffused a large number of crops and technologies from Spain into medieval Europe, where farming was mostly restricted to wheat strains obtained much earlier via central Asia. Watson listed eighteen crops, including sorghum from Africa, citrus fruits from China, and numerous crops from India such as mangos, rice, cotton and sugar cane, which were distributed throughout Islamic lands that, according to Watson, had previously not grown them. Watson argued that these introductions, along with an increased mechanization of agriculture, led to major changes in economy, population distribution, vegetation cover, agricultural production and income, population levels, urban growth, the distribution of the labour force, linked industries, cooking, diet and clothing in the Islamic world. Also transmitted via Muslim influence, a silk industry flourished, flax was cultivated and linen exported, and esparto grass, which grew wild in the more arid parts, was collected and turned into various articles.[194] However Michael Decker has challenged significant parts of Watson's thesis, including whether all these crops were introduced to Europe during this period. Decker used literary and archaeological evidence to suggest that four of the listed crops (i.e. durum wheat, Asiatic rice, sorghum and cotton) were common centuries before the Islamic period, that the crops which were new were not as important as Watson had suggested, and generally arguing that Islamic agricultural practices in areas such as irrigation were more of an evolution from those of the ancient world than the revolution suggested by Watson.[195]

The production of sugar from sugar cane,[196] water clocks, pulp and paper, silk, and various advances in making perfume, were transferred from the Islamic world to medieval Europe.[197] Fulling mills and advances in mill technology may have also been transmitted from the Islamic world to medieval Europe,[198] along with the large-scale use of inventions like the suction pump,[199] noria and chain pumps for irrigation purposes. According to Watson, "The Islamic contribution was less in the invention of new devices than in the application on a much wider scale of devices which in pre-Islamic times had been used only over limited areas and to a limited extent."[200] These innovations made it possible for some industrial operations that were previously served by manual labour or draught animals to be driven by machinery in medieval Europe.[201]

Coinage

While the earliest coins were minted and widely circulated in Europe, and Ancient Rome, Islamic coinage had some influence on Medieval European minting. The 8th-century English king Offa of Mercia minted a near-copy of Abbasid dinars struck in 774 by Caliph Al-Mansur with "Offa Rex" centered on the reverse.[202] The moneyer visibly had little understanding of Arabic, as the Arabic text contains a number of errors.

In Sicily, Malta and Southern Italy from about 913 tarì gold coins of Islamic origin were minted in great number by the Normans, Hohenstaufens and the early Angevins rulers.[203] When the Normans invaded Sicily in the 12th century, they issued tarì coins bearing legends in Arabic and Latin.[204] The tarìs were so widespread that imitations were made in southern Italy (Amalfi and Salerno) which only used illegible "pseudo-Kufic" imitations of Arabic.[205,206]

According to Janet Abu-Lughod:

Figure 73: *Tarì gold coin of Roger II of Sicily, with Arabic inscriptions, minted in Palermo. British Museum.*

The preferred specie for international transactions before the 13th century, in Europe as well as the Middle East and even India, were the gold coins struck by Byzantium and then Egypt. It was not until after the 13th century that some Italian cities (Florence and Genoa) began to mint their own gold coins, but these were used to supplement rather than supplant the Middle Eastern coins already in circulation.[207]

Literature

It was first suggested by Miguel Asín Palacios in 1919 that Dante Alighieri's *Divine Comedy*, considered the greatest epic of Italian literature, derived many features of and episodes about the hereafter directly or indirectly from Arabic works on Islamic eschatology, such as the *Hadith* and the spiritual writings of Ibn Arabi. The *Kitab al-Miraj*, concerning Muhammad's ascension to Heaven, was translated into Latin in 1264 or shortly before[208] as *Liber Scale Machometi*, "The Book of Muhammad's Ladder". Dante was certainly aware of Muslim philosophy, naming Avicenna and Averroes last in his list of non-Christian philosophers in Limbo, alongside the great Greek and Latin philosophers. How strong the similarities are to *Kitab al-Miraj* remains a matter of

Islamic world contributions to Medieval Europe 97

Figure 74: *A gold dinar of the English king Offa of Mercia, a copy of the dinars of the Abbasid Caliphate (774). It combines the Latin legend OFFA REX with Arabic legends. British Museum.*

Figure 75: *Crusader coins of the Kingdom of Jerusalem. Left: Denier in European style with Holy Sepulchre. Middle: One of the first Kingdom of Jerusalem gold coins, copying Islamic dinars. Right: Gold coin after 1250, with Christian symbols following Papal complaints. British Museum.*

scholarly debate however, with no clear evidence that Dante was in fact influenced.

Sources

- Attar, Samar (2007), *The vital roots of European enlightenment : Ibn Tufayl's influence on modern Western thought*, Lanham: Lexington Books, ISBN 0-7391-1989-3
- Badr, Gamal Moursi (Spring 1978), "Islamic Law: Its Relation to Other Legal Systems", *The American Journal of Comparative Law*, The American Journal of Comparative Law, Vol. 26, No. 2, **26** (2 [Proceedings of an International Conference on Comparative Law, Salt Lake City, Utah, February 24–25, 1977]): 187–198, doi: 10.2307/839667[209], JSTOR 839667[210]
- Cardini, Franco. *Europe and Islam*. Blackwell Publishing, 2001. ISBN 978-0-631-22637-6
- Farmer, Henry George (1988), *Historical facts for the Arabian Musical Influence*, Ayer Publishing, ISBN 0-405-08496-X, OCLC 220811631[211]
- Frieder, Braden K. *Chivalry & the perfect prince: tournaments, art, and armor at the Spanish Habsburg court* Truman State University, 2008 ISBN 1-931112-69-X, ISBN 978-1-931112-69-7
- Grierson, Philip *Medieval European Coinage* Cambridge University Press, 2007 ISBN 0-521-03177-X, ISBN 978-0-521-03177-6
- Hobson, John M. (2004), *The Eastern Origins of Western Civilisation*, Cambridge: Cambridge Univ. Press, ISBN 0-521-54724-5
- Lebedel, Claude (2006), *Les Croisades, origines et conséquences*, Editions Ouest-France, ISBN 2-7373-4136-1, OCLC 181885553[212]
- Lewis, Bernard (1993), *Les Arabes dans l'histoire*, Flammarion, ISBN 2-08-081362-5, OCLC 36229500[213]
- Mack, Rosamond E. Bazaar to Piazza: Islamic Trade and Italian Art, 1300–1600, University of California Press, 2001 ISBN 0-520-22131-1, google books[214]
- Makdisi, John A. (June 1999), "The Islamic Origins of the Common Law", *North Carolina Law Review*, **77** (5): 1635–1739
- Matthew, Donald, *The Norman kingdom of Sicily* Cambridge University Press, 1992 ISBN 978-0-521-26911-7
- Roux, Jean-Paul (1985), *Les explorateurs au Moyen-Age*, Hachette, ISBN 2-01-279339-8
- Watt, W. Montgomery (2004), *The influence of Islam on medieval Europe*, Edinburgh: Edinburgh University Press, ISBN 0-7486-0517-7

External links

- Zalta, Edward N. (ed.). "Influence of Arabic and Islamic Philosophy on the Latin West"[215]. *Stanford Encyclopedia of Philosophy*.
- Islamic Contributions to the West[216] by Rachida El Diwani, Professor of Comparative Literature.
- "How Greek Science Passed to the Arabs"[217] by De Lacy O'Leary
- Islamic Contributions to Civilization[218] by Stanwood Cobb (1963)

Reception of Islam in Early Modern Europe

Left image: *The School of Athens* by Raphael, a symbol of Renaissance knowledge, includes Muslim Averroes in its community of learned men.
Right image: Averroes and Pythagoras (detail).

There was a certain amount of cultural contact between Europe in the Renaissance to Early Modern period and the Islamic world (at the time primarily represented by the Ottoman Empire and, geographically more remote, Safavid Persia), however decreasing in intensity after medieval cultural contact in the era of the crusades and the *Reconquista*.

European contact with Islam has been mostly limited with the military effort opposing the expansion of the Ottoman Empire. There was limited direct interaction between the two cultures even though there was plenty of trade between Europe and the Middle East at this time. Merchants would often deal through an intermediary,[219] a practice common since the time of the Roman

Empire. Historians have noted that even during the 12th and 14th centuries the two parties had little interest in learning about each other.[220]

The history of the Ottoman Empire is intimately connected to the history of Renaissance and Early Modern Europe. The European Renaissance was significantly triggered by the Fall of Constantinople in 1453 (resulting in a wave of Byzantine scholars fleeing to Italy). The Ottoman Empire reached its historical apogee in 1566, coinciding with the beginning of the scientific revolution in Europe, which would lead to the political dominance of emerging modern Europe over the course of the following century.

Iberian peninsula

Granada was the last stronghold of the region of Spain known as Andalusia, which was considered Wikipedia:Manual of Style/Words to watch#Unsupported attributions a pinnacle of culture in the western Muslim Empire.[221] Trade from Granada included silk, ceramic, and porcelain. From 1230 until its fall to the Christians, the city was under the rule of the Nasrid dynasty.[222] Ferdinand III of Castile had conquered all Andalusia by 1251.[223] It was not until after the 1469 marriage between Prince Ferdinand II of Aragon and Isabella I of Castile that Alhambra, the Nasrid palace of Granada, fell to Spanish forces.[224] Alhambra fell to the combined forces of Isabella and Ferdinand on January 2, 1492.[225]

Alhambra was known Wikipedia:Manual of Style/Words to watch#Unsupported attributions as one of the greatest achievements of urban art in the Muslim world during the time of the Nasrids.[226] The Court of the Myrtles and the Court of the Lions are the only two portions of the palace to survive to present time.[227]

Reception of Islam in Early Modern England

The first English convert to Islam mentioned by name is John Nelson.[228] 16th century writer Richard Hakluyt claimed he was forced to convert, though he mentions in the same story other Englishmen who had converted willingly.Wikipedia:Citation needed

> This king had a son which was a ruler in an island called Gerbi, whereunto arrived an English ship called the Green Dragon, of the which was master one M. Blonket, who, having a very unhappy boy on that ship, and understanding that whosoever would turn Turk should be well entertained of the a yeoman of our Queen's guard, whom the king's son had enforced to turn Turk; his name was John Nelson.[229]

Figure 76: *Portrait of Abd el-Ouahed ben Messaoud, a Moorish ambassador to Queen Elizabeth I in 1600*

Captain John Ward of Kent was one of a number of British sailors who became pirates based in the Maghreb who also converted to Islam (see also Barbary pirates). Later, some Unitarians became interested in the faith, and Henry Stubbes wrote so favourably about Islam that it is thought he too had converted to the faith.Wikipedia:Citation needed

From 1609 to 1616, England lost 466 ships to Barbary pirates, who sold the passengers into slavery in North Africa.[230] In 1625, it was reported that Lundy, an island in the Bristol Channel which had been a pirate lair for much of the previous half century, had been occupied by three Ottoman pirates who were threatening to burn Ilfracombe; Algerine rovers were using the island as a base in 1635, although the island had itself been attacked and plundered by a Spanish raid in 1633.[231] In 1627, Barbary pirates under command of the Dutch renegade Jan Janszoon operating from the Moroccan port of Salé occupied Lundy. During this time there were reports of captured slaves being sent to Algiers and of the Islamic flag flying over Lundy.

Ottoman presence in the Balkans

The Ottoman Empire emerged in 1299 and lasted until 1919. The Ottomans were strong proponents of Sunni Islam.[232] In the 13th century, the kingdom was only in a small portion of northwest Anatolia but by the 16th century, it expanded to the heartland of the Byzantine Empire and its capital, Constantinople. The height of the Ottoman Empire occurred under the sultans Selim the Grim, also known as Selim I (1512–1520) and Suleyman the Magnificent (1520–1566). Under their reigns, the Turks conquered Egypt, Syria, and the North coast of Africa, the Red Sea, the island of Rhodes, and the Balkans all the way to the Great Hungarian Plain.

Many members of Kosovo's higher class, such as the Serbs and the Vlachs, converted to Islam during the Dušan period (1331–1355). A large part of the reason for the conversion was probably economic and social, as Muslims had considerably more rights and privileges than Christian subjects. As a result, Kosovo's three largest towns were majority Muslim by 1485, where Christians had once formed a dense population before the rise of the Ottoman Empire. The movement was effective due to the wandering of Sufis who traveled around the region teaching religion as they went. By the 16th century, towns like Prizren, Skopje, and Đakovica had established centers of learning that became crucial in inspiring and educating scholars who would then use their knowledge to benefit the Ottoman Empire and the Muslim world. From this time onward, many books circulated in the region that had a Persian influence while written in the Albanian language and Arabic alphabet. The oldest genre in this style is known as *Bejtexhinji* poetry.[233]

Slavery

Slavery at the time of the European Renaissance was a socio-economic factor especially around the Mediterranean Sea region. It was accepted and approved for both Muslims and Christians. Most slaves came from warfare, privateering, or the international slave trade. Only some of the Arabian slaves in Europe were Muslims by origin.[234] Many of the Muslim slaves were baptized before they were sold for the first time and then were given a new Christian name. There were, however, some Muslims who were not baptized and who kept their original names, but if they had children the newborns were immediately baptized. Most Muslim slaves converted to Christianity because there was hard social pressure at the time for them to convert. They also improved their social position by converting to Christianity, such as they would rise from a slave to a serf.[235]

There were a small percentage of learned Muslim captives who were among the intellectual elite in their original hometowns among the Muslim prisoners

Figure 77: *Portrait assumed to be of Leo Africanus (Sebastiano del Piombo, around 1520)*

and slaves. Captured Muslim scientists, physicians, and copyists were in high demand at slave markets. Learned Muslim captives were held in high regard by the authorities and they were sold for very high prices. They were wanted for the knowledge and advancements the Arabs had made over the Europeans. Copyists of Arabic manuscripts were needed in Spain to translate Arabic texts for the practice of medicine, the study of Arabic philosophy, and because of the popular interest in Europe for the translations of Arabic scientific texts. Learned Muslim captives played a very important role in the spread of Arabic science and philosophy over the Christian world.[236]

The liberation of Muslim slaves was a state affair and elevated the popular esteem of the sovereign government. Muslim slaves were either freed or exchanged through special legislation and international treaties.[237]

Examples of learned Muslim captives

One account of a highly esteemed Muslim slave is of Moroccan geographer al-Hassan al-Wazzan al-Fasi, who made important contributions to geography and Italian texts. In 1519, al-Fasi was captured by a group of Sicilian pirates while he was on his way home from Egypt. When he was picked up he had scholarly notes on him that he had made from his travels through Africa. The pirates soon realized his value and they gave him to Pope Leo X in Rome. Al-Fasi was baptized on June 6, 1520, and renamed Joannis Leo, but he became known as Leo the African or Leo Africanus. Leo Africanus learned Italian, taught in Barcelona, and made Arabic notes in a book called Description of Africa, which was used for many years as an important source of geographic information on Muslim Africa.

Barbary pirates

The Barbary States, who were allies of the Ottoman Empire, sent Barbary pirates to raid parts of Western Europe in order to capture Christian slaves to sell at slave markets in the Arab World throughout the Renaissance period. Contemporaneous accounts suggest that a population of about 35,000 European slaves was maintained on the Barbary Coast. One writer estimates, on the basis that about 8,500 fresh slaves per annum would be required to maintain such a population, that as many as 1.25 million Europeans may have been taken in the 250 years to 1780, though there are no records to confirm such numbers. The slaves were captured mainly from seaside villages in Italy, Spain and Portugal, and from farther places like France or England, the Netherlands, Ireland and even Iceland and North America, ultimately provoking the First Barbary War of the newly-formed United States.

Early Modern Orientalism

Following the first wave of Arabic interest during the Renaissance of the 12th century, which saw numerous Arabic texts being translated into Latin, there was a 'second wave' of interest in the study of Arabic literature, Arabic science and Islamic philosophy in 16th-century France and 17th-century England.

Together with the development of the Franco-Ottoman alliance, cultural and scientific exchanges between France and the Ottoman Empire flourished. French scholars such as Guillaume Postel or Pierre Belon were able to travel to Asia Minor and the Middle East to collect information.[238]

Scientific exchange is thought to have occurred, as numerous works in Arabic, especially pertaining to astronomy were brought back, annotated and studied by scolars such as Guillaume Postel. Transmission of scientific knowledge, such as the Tusi-couple, may have occurred on such occasions, at the time when Copernicus was establishing his own astronomical theories.[239]

Books, such as the Coran, were brought back to be integrated in Royal libraries, such as the *Bibliothèque Royale de Fontainebleau*, to create a foundation for the *Collège des lecteurs royaux*, future Collège de France. French novels and tragedies were written with the Ottoman Empire as a theme or background.

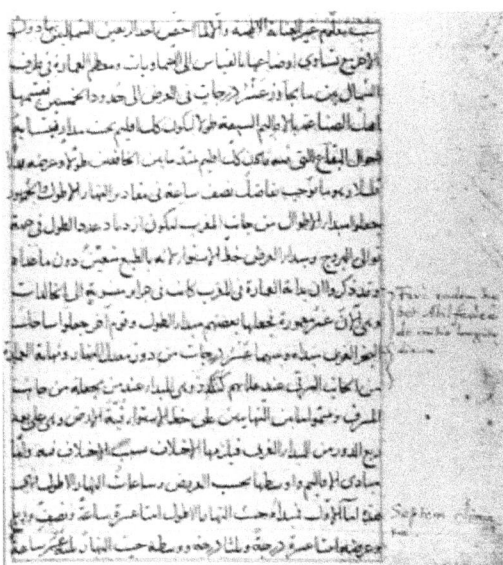

Figure 78: *Arabic astronomical manuscript of Nasir al-Din al-Tusi, annotated by Guillaume Postel.*

In 1561, Gabriel Bounin published *La Soltane*, a tragedy highlighting the role of Roxelane in the 1553 execution of Mustapha, the elder son of Suleiman.[240] This tragedy marks the first time the Ottomans were introduced on stage in France.[241]

Arabic manuscripts were considered the key to a 'treasure house' of ancient knowledge, which led to the founding of Arabic Chairs at Oxford and Cambridge Universities, where Arabic was taught. A large collection of Arabic manuscripts were acquired, collected in places such as the Bodleian Library at Oxford. These Arabic manuscripts were sought after by natural philosophers for their research in subjects such as mathematics and observational astronomy, and also encompassed subjects ranging from science, religion, and medicine, to typography and garden plants.

Besides scientific and philosophical literature, works of Arabic fiction were also translated into Latin and English during the 17th and 18th centuries. The most famous one was the *One Thousand and One Nights* (*Arabian Nights*), which was first translated into English in 1706 and has since then had a profound influence on English literature. Another famous work was Ibn Tufail's philosophical novel[242,243] *Hayy ibn Yaqdhan*, which was translated into Latin as *Philosophus Autodidactus* by Edward Pococke the Younger in 1671 and

Figure 79: *Ottoman Empire Coran, copied circa 1536, bound according to regulations set under Francis I circa 1549, with arms of Henri II. Bibliothèque Nationale de France.*

then into English by Simon Ockley in 1708. The English translation of *Hayy ibn Yaqdhan*, set on a desert island, may have inspired Daniel Defoe to write *Robinson Crusoe*, considered the first novel in English, in 1719.[244,245,246,247] Later translated literary works include *Layla and Majnun* and Ibn al-Nafis' *Theologus Autodidactus*.

Left image: A "Bellini type" Islamic prayer rug, seen from the top, at the feet of the Virgin Mary, in Gentile Bellini's *Madonna and Child Enthroned*, late 15th century, an example of Oriental carpets in Renaissance painting.
Right image: Prayer rug, Anatolia, late 15th to early 16th century, with "reentrant" keyhole motif.

The Muslim Moors had a noticeable influence on the works of George Peele and William Shakespeare. Some of their works featured Moorish characters, such as Peele's *The Battle of Alcazar* and Shakespeare's *The Merchant of Venice*, *Titus Andronicus* and *Othello*, which featured a Moorish Othello as its title character. These works are said to have been inspired by several Moorish delegations from Morocco to Elizabethan England around 1600.[248] A portrait was painted of one of the Moorish ambassadors, Abd el-Ouahed ben Messaoud ben Mohammed Anoun, who had come to promote an Anglo-Moroccan alliance.

At the Bodleian Library of Oxford University, there were hundreds of Arabic manuscripts, as well as dozens of Persian and Turkish ones, available during the 17th century. These included works on Islamic law and Arabic grammar; the lexicography of Al-Firuzabadi and Al-Jawhari; works on Arabic poetry; the Indian literary work *Kalila and Dimna*; the proverbs of Al-Maydani and *Maqama* of Al-Hariri of Basra; the medical works of Al-Razi, Avicenna, Ibn al-Baitar, Hunayn ibn Ishaq, Al-Majusi, Ibn al-Jazzar, Abu al-Qasim al-Zahrawi, Ibn Zuhr, Maimonides and Ibn al-Nafis; the astronomical works of Ibn al-Banna, Ibn al-Shatir, Al-Farghani and Alhazen; the *Masudic Canon* by Abu Rayhan Biruni and the *Book of Fixed Stars* by Al-Sufi; several Ottoman scientific works by Taqi al-Din Muhammad ibn Ma'ruf; occult and alchemical works; the *Secretum Secretorum*; Al-Safadi's biographical dictionary *Al-Sihah*; the historical works of Al-Tabari, Al-Isfahani, Al-Makin, Ibn Khallikan, Al-Dhahabi, Al-Waqidi, Ibn al-Shina, Al-Utbi, Ibn al-Jawzi, Ibn al-Athir, Sibt ibn al-Jawzi, Ibn Abi Usaibia, Bar-Hebraeus, Al-Tunaynai, Ibn

Figure 80: *Suleiman the Magnificent appears at the table in the 1563 The Wedding at Cana by Paolo Veronese.*

Duqmaq, Ibn Taghribirdi, Al-Suyuti, Al-Jannabi, Ibn Hayyan, Ibn Miskawayh, Ibn Hajar al-Asqalani and Al-Maqrizi; the *History of Time* by Al-Masudi and volume five of Ibn Khaldun's historiographical work *Kitab al-Ibar*; the historical and geographical works of Abu al-Fida; the *Sahih al-Bukhari* and Qur'anic commentaries; the *Algebra* by Al-Khwarizmi and the mathematical works of Nasir al-Din al-Tusi; the *Encyclopedia of the Brethren of Purity* and Avienna's *The Book of Healing*; the works of Ibn Bajjah and Ibn Tufail; geographical works of Ibn Khordadbeh and Ibn Hawqal; . A Latin translation of two of Ali Qushji's works, the *Tract on Arithmetic* and *Tract on Astronomy*, was published by John Greaves in 1650.[249]

The turban in art and politics

The turban often represented Muslims in the paintings of Italian and Flemish artists when they depicted scenes of the Ottoman Empire and Biblical lore. Famous figures such as Suleyman the Magnificent, Hagar, and Hayreddin Barbarossa appear in these paintings. The tradition of depicting Biblical characters in turbans has continued through to this century, as at least one of the wise men is always depicted with a turban.[250]

Turban iconography was highly prominent, especially in Renaissance England. While friendly relations were formed between England and the Islamic civilization of the Middle East in the early 16th century, Turkish fashions became popular for the higher classes. During times of interaction with Istanbul, Queen Elizabeth I of England wore Turkish clothing styles. It was believed that she favored working with the Islamic sultans of Istanbul rather than the Roman Catholic leaders of Europe. These suspicions were heightened when she asked Sultan Murad III and his son Mohammad III for military assistance. Although she never did receive any assistance from the sultans, her relations with the Sultan and his son did not waver.[251]

Views on Muslim women

Alexander Ross, a writer and controversialist living in the first half of the 17th century, praised the Turks for being "more modest in their conversation generally than we; Men and Women converse not together promiscuously, as among us."[252] Ross believed that England could learn a great deal from the Muslims. During the Renaissance, English women disrespected their husbands because they were free to do what they wanted, which society believed led to a moral deterioration.Wikipedia:Accuracy dispute#Disputed statement[253] European women also began leaving home to become male-like figures in society. Other European women attacked male chauvinism and defended the status of women by handing out pamphlets. Women rebelled against male religious hierarchy and began to replace men as preachers and pastors.[254] Christian writers highly admired Muslim women because they were frugal compared to English women, they were respected by their husbands because they did not play "false" with them, and because Muslim women went immediately back to work after giving birth and they still had time to raise their children themselves, unlike English women.[255]Wikipedia:Citation needed

The Muslim model became an example of the "exotic" and "Utopian" ideal because it was not possible in European society.[256] European men sought to reinforce the traditional role of women and wanted their women to adhere to the model of Muslim women as frugal, obedient, wearing modest apparel, and respectful towards their husbands. Muslims and Englishmen differed in various ways, especially in their religious beliefs and militarism, but they did agree with each other on the representation of Muslim women.

Appendix

References

[1] Hourani 2002, p. 42.
[2] Manfred, W: "International Journal of Middle East Studies", pages 59-79, Vol. 12, No. 1. Middle East Studies Association of North America, Aug 1980.
[3] Hill, Donald. *Islamic Science and Engineering*. 1993. Edinburgh Univ. Press. , p.4
[4] Islamic art and architecture http://www.history.com/encyclopedia.do?vendorId=FWNE.fw. .is045900.a#FWNE.fw..is045900.a History.com
[5] Carole Hillenbrand. *The Crusades: Islamic perspectives*, Routledge, 2000, p. 386
[6] Hillenbrand, p. 388
[7] Savory; p. 195-8
[8] Hyman and Walsh *Philosophy in the Middle Ages* Indianapolis, 3rd edition, p. 216
[9] Meri, Josef W. and Jere L. Bacharach, Editors, *Medieval Islamic Civilization* Vol.1, A - K, Index, 2006, p. 451
[10] Hourani 2002, p. 41.
[11] Milton, G (2005) White Gold: The Extraordinary Story of Thomas Pellow And Islam's One Million White Slaves, Sceptre, London
[12] " The Crimean Tatars and their Russian-Captive Slaves http://www2.econ.hit-u.ac.jp/~areastd/ mediterranean/mw/pdf/18/10.pdf" (PDF). Eizo Matsuki, *Mediterranean Studies Group at Hitotsubashi University.*
[13] " Historical survey > Slave societies http://www.britannica.com/blackhistory/article-24157". Encyclopædia Britannica,
[14] Vikings in the East, Remarkable Eyewitness Accounts http://www.nordicway.com/search/ Vikings%20in%20the%20East.htm
[15] Basgoz, I. & Wilson, H. E. (1989), The educational tradition of the Ottoman Empire and the development of the Turkish educational system of the republican era. Turkish Review 3(16), 15
[16] The preaching of Islam: history of the propagation of the Muslim faith By Sir Thomas Walker Arnold, pp. 135-144
[17] as quoted in , pg. 158
[18] Pew 2011.
[19] by example only 6% of the Russian population is Islamic http://www.kommersant.ru/doc/ 1997068
[20] 2011 Albanian census http://www.instat.gov.al/media/177358/njoftim_per_media_-_fjala_e_ drejtorit_te_instat_ines_nurja_per_rezultatet_finale_te_census_2011.pdf
[21] *"Religious Composition by Country, 2010-2050" http://www.pewforum.org/2015/04/02/ religious-projection-table/2010/percent/all/* in: *Pew Research Center*, Retrieved 10 November 2016
[22] *Republic of Macedonia http//www.globalreligiousfutures.org*, in: *Pew-Templeton Global Religious Futures*, Retrieved 10 November 2016
[23] *Census of Pupulation, Households and Dwellings in the Republic of Macedonia, 2002*, p. 518 http://www.stat.gov.mk/publikacii/knigaIX.pdf
[24] 2013 Census, http://popis2013.ba/
[25] For the purpose of the chart, the categories 'Islam' and 'Muslims' were merged.
[26] The rise of Russian Muslims worries Orthodox Church http://www.timesonline.co.uk/tol/news/ world/article551693.ece, The Times, 5 August 2005
[27] Don Melvin, "Europe works to assimilate Muslims" http://www.ajc.com/news/content/news/ stories/1204/17muslims.html, *Atlanta Journal-Constitution*, 2004-12-17
[28] Tolerance and fear collide in the Netherlands http://www.unhcr.org/publ/PUBL/40ffd2eb4. html, UNHCR, Refugees Magazine, Issue 135 (New Europe)
[29] Philip Jenkins, " Demographics, Religion, and the Future of Europe http://deathandreligion. plamienok.sk/files/21-Demographics_Religion_and_the_Future_of_Europe.pdf", *Orbis: A Journal of World Affairs*, vol. 50, no. 3, pp. 533, summer 2006

[30] Mary Mederios Kent, *Do Muslims have more children than other women in western Europe?* http://www.prb.org/Articles/2008/muslimsineurope.aspx?p=1 http://www.prb.org/Articles/2008/muslimsineurope.aspxhttp://www.prb.org/Publications/Articles/2008/muslimsineurope.aspx, Population Reference Bureau, February 2008, Simon Kuper, *Head count belies vision of 'Eurabia'* http://www.ft.com/cms/s/0/123ade02-4e6f-11dc-85e7-0000779fd2ac,print=yes.html, Financial Times, 19 August 2007, Doug Saunders, *The 'Eurabia' myth deserves a debunking* https://www.theglobeandmail.com/servlet/story/RTGAM.20080920.wreckoning20/BNStory/International/home/ http://dougsaunders.net/2008/09/eurabia-debunking-steyn-bawer-melanie-phillips-geert-wilders/http://dougsaunders.tumblr.com/post/7999134091/debunking-the-eurabia-myth, The Globe and Mail, 20 September 2008, *Islam and demography: A waxing crescent* http://www.economist.com/node/18008022/print, The Economist, 27 January 2011

[31] Esther Pan, *Europe: Integrating Islam* http://www.cfr.org/publication/8252/europe.html, Council on Foreign Relations, 2005-07-13

[32] Albanian census 2011 http://www.instat.gov.al/media/177354/main_results__population_and_housing_census_2011.pdf

[33] More Orthodox Christians than Muslims in Italy http://www.ismu.org/2016/07/in-italia-ortodossi-piu-numerosi-dei-musulmani/

[34] //en.wikipedia.org/w/index.php?title=Template:Islamophobia&action=edit

[35] European Monitoring Centre on Racism and Xenophobia (2006): Muslims in the European Union. Discrimination and Islamophobia http://fra.europa.eu/sites/default/files/fra_uploads/156-Manifestations_EN.pdf Retrieved September 25, 2012

[36] http://press.princeton.edu/titles/9068.html

[37] http://journals.openedition.org/assr/18403#ftn5

[38] https://web.archive.org/web/20110209094904/http://www.pewforum.org/The-Future-of-the-Global-Muslim-Population.aspx

[39] http://features.pewforum.org/muslim-population/

[40] http://ssrn.com/abstract=1574982

[41] http://news.bbc.co.uk/2/hi/in_depth/europe/2005/muslims_in_europe/

[42] http://www.khabrein.info/index.php?option=com_content&task=view&id=14172&Itemid=88

[43] http://euro-islam.info/

[44] http://www.euro-islam.info/2013/01/23/the-numbers-of-french-muslims-and-muslims-in-france-are-exaggerated/

[45] http://bibliobs.nouvelobs.com/essais/20121220.OBS3294/on-exagere-deliberement-le-nombre-de-musulmans-en-france.html

[46] https://ideas.repec.org/p/iza/izadps/dp4459.html

[47] https://ideas.repec.org/b/erv/ebooks/b001.html

[48] http://hanskoechler.com/ice.htm

[49] http://www.nypl.org/blog/2011/12/15/islam-europe-resource-guide

[50] The Arabs called the latter *Muwalladun* or *Muladi*. Menocal http://www.barnesandnoble.com/sample/read/9780316092791 (2002). *Ornament of the World*, p. 16

[51] Richard A Fletcher, Moorish Spain https://books.google.com/books?id=wrMG-LfuU7oC&printsec=frontcover#v=onepage&q=false (University of California Press, 2006), pp.1,19.

[52] Ross Brann, "The Moors?" http://drum.lib.umd.edu/bitstream/1903/12049/1/Ramos_umd_0117E_12042.pdf, *Andalusia*, New York University. Quote: "Andalusi Arabic sources, as opposed to later Mudéjar and Morisco sources in Aljamiado and medieval Spanish texts, neither refer to individuals as Moors nor recognize any such group, community or culture."

[53] Menocal, María Rosa (2002). *Ornament of the World: How Muslims, Jews and Christians Created a Culture of Tolerance in Medieval Spain*. Little, Brown, & Co. , p. 241

[54] Pieris, P.E. *Ceylon and the Hollanders 1658-1796* https://archive.org/stream/ceylonhollanders00pieruoft#page/n5/mode/2up. American Ceylon Mission Press, Tellippalai Ceylon 1918

[55] "Here dwell a people called by the Greeks Maurusii, and by the Romans and the natives Mauri" Strabo, *Geographica* 17.3.2. Lewis and Short, *Latin Dictionary*, 1879 s.v. "Mauri" http://www.perseus.tufts.edu/hopper/text?doc=Perseus%3Atext%3A1999.04.0059%3Aentry%3DMauri

[56] Cornelius Tacitus, Arthur Murphy, The Historical Annals of Cornelius Tacitus: With Supplements, Volume 1 (D. Neall, 1829) p114 https//books.google.com.
[57] For an introduction to the culture of the *Azawagh Arabs*, see Rebecca Popenoe, *Feeding Desire — Fatness, Beauty and Sexuality among a Saharan People*. Routledge, London (2003)
[58] DRAE http://dle.rae.es/
[59] Lodovico Sforza http://www.bookrags.com/biography/lodovico-sforza/, in: Thomas Gale, Encyclopedia of World Biography, 2005–2006
[60] Xosé Manuel González Reboredo, *Leyendas Gallegas de Tradición Oral* (Galician Legends of the Oral Tradition) https//books.google.com, Galicia: Editorial Galaxia, 2004, p. 18, Googlebooks, accessed 12 Jul 2010
[61] Rodney Gallop, *Portugal: A Book of Folkways* https://books.google.com/books?id=uQ88AAAAIAAJ&printsec=frontcover&dq=PORTUGAL:+A+BOOK+OF+FOLKWAYS#PPA77,M1, Cambridge University Press (CUP), 1936; reprint CUP Archives, 1961, Googlebooks, accessed 12 Jul 2010.
[62] Francisco Martins Sarmento, "A Mourama" http://www.csarmento.uminho.pt/docs/ndat/rg/RG100_11.pdf, in *Revista de Guimaraes*, No. 100, 1990, Centro de Estudos de Património, Universidade do Minho, accessed 12 Jul 2010
[63] Euskadi.net http://www1.euskadi.net/morris/resultado.asp
[64] A. Hussein 'From where did the moors come from? http://www.lankalibrary.com/cul/muslims/moors.htm
[65] Rodd, Francis. "Kahena, Queen of the Berbers:" A Sketch of the Arab Invasion of Ifriqiya in the First Century of the Hijra" Bulletin of the School of Oriental Studies, University of London, Vol. 3, No. 4, (1925), 731-2
[66] Lapidus, 200-201
[67] Ibn Hazm, طوق الحمامة
[68] Ronald Segal, *Islam's Black Slaves* (2003), Atlantic Books,
[69] Granada http://jewishencyclopedia.com/view.jsp?artid=412&letter=G&search=Granada by Richard Gottheil, Meyer Kayserling, *Jewish Encyclopedia*. 1906 ed.
[70] See *History of Al-Andalus*.
[71] Adams et al., "The Genetic Legacy of Religious Diversity and Intolerance: Paternal Lineages of Christians, Jews, and Muslims in the Iberian Peninsula" http://www.cell.com/AJHG/abstract/S0002-9297%2808%2900592-2, *Cell*, 2008. Quote: "Admixture analysis based on binary and Y-STR haplotypes indicates a high mean proportion of ancestry from North African (10.6%) ranging from zero in Gascony to 21.7% in Northwest Castile."
[72] Elena Bosch, "The religious conversions of Jews and Muslims have had a profound impact on the population of the Iberian Peninsula" http://www.upf.edu/enoticies/home_upf_en/1206.html , Universitat Pompeu Fabra, 2008, Quote: "The study shows that religious conversions and the subsequent marriages between people of different lineage had a relevant impact on modern populations both in Spain, especially in the Balearic Islands, and in Portugal."
[73] Richard Fletcher. *Moorish Spain* p. 10. University of California Press, 1993.
[74] Curl p. 502.
[75] Pevsner, *The Penguin Dictionary of Architecture*.
[76] In his July 15, 2005 blog article "Is that a Moor's head?" https://archive.is/20120708120756/http://findarticles.com/p/articles/mi_m1252/is_13_132/ai_n27858944/, Mathew N. Schmalz refers to a discussion on the American Heraldry Society's website where at least one participant described the moor's head as a "potentially explosive image".
[77] G. Mokhtar. *General History of Africa: Ancient Civilizations of Africa*, p. 427.
[78] https://books.google.com/books?id=nQbylEdqJKkC&printsec=frontcover#v=onepage&q&f=false
[79] http://www.nyu.edu/gsas/program/neareast/andalusia/pdf/10.pdf
[80] https://www.pbs.org/wgbh/pages/frontline/shows/secret/famous/ssecretum1.html
[81] http://www.britannica.com/EBchecked/topic/391449/Moor
[82] https://web.archive.org/web/20080313043250/http://www.usp.nus.edu.sg/post/morocco/literature/amine2.html
[83] http://www.vam.ac.uk/content/articles/a/africans-in-medieval-and-renaissance-art-moors-head/

[84] https://web.archive.org/web/20080419095235/http://www.folger.edu/eduLesPlanDtl.cfm?lpid=573

[85] //en.wikipedia.org/w/index.php?title=Template:History_of_al-Andalus&action=edit

[86] "Para los autores árabes medievales, el término Al-Andalus designa la totalidad de las zonas conquistadas — siquiera temporalmente — por tropas arabo-musulmanas en territorios actualmente pertenecientes a Portugal, España y Francia" ("For medieval Arab authors, Al-Andalus designated all the conquered areas — even temporarily —by Arab-Muslim troops in territories now belonging to Portugal, Spain and France"), José Ángel García de Cortázar, *V Semana de Estudios Medievales: Nájera, 1 al 5 de agosto de 1994*, Gobierno de La Rioja, Instituto de Estudios Riojanos, 1995, p.52.

[87] O'Callaghan, Joseph F., *A History of Medieval Spain*, Cornell University Press, 1983, p.142

[88] Lewis, Bernard. The Jews of Islam. PrincetMeyrick, Fredrick. The Doctrine of the Church of England on the Holy Communion.on, NJ: Princeton University Press, 1984.pg. 14. "Under the ruling Caliph (the descendant of Mohammed–the prophet of G-d on earth), the Jews were able to preserve their rites and traditions. Peaceful coexistence led to their economic and social expansion. Their status was that of Dhimmis, non-Muslims living in a land governed by Muslims. The Jews had limited autonomy, but full rights to practice their religion, as well as full protection by their Muslim rulers, but this did not occur for free. There was a specific tax called the jizya that Dhimmis had to pay to receive these benefits. Having its origin in the Qur'an, it states Dhimmis who did not pay this tax, should either convert to Islam, or face the death penalty (Qur'an 9, 29). This tax, higher than the tax Muslims had to pay, was in several occasions one of the most important sources of income for the kingdom. The jizya was not only a tax, but also a symbolic expression of subordination (Lewis 14)."It is a common misapprehension that the holy war meant that the Muslims gave their opponents a choice 'between Islam and the sword'. This was sometimes the case, but only when the opponents were polytheist and idol-worshippers. For Jews, Christians, and other 'People of the Book', there was a third possibility, they might become a 'protected group', paying a tax or tribute to the Muslims but enjoying internal autonomy" (Watt 144)

[89] Specifically, 27,000 Syrian troops were composed of 6,000 men from each of the four main Syrian *junds* of Jund Dimashq (Damascus), Jund Hims (Homs), Jund al-Urdunn (Jordan), and Jund Filastin (Filastin), plus 3,000 from Jund Qinnasrin. An additional 3,000 were picked up in Egypt. See R. Dozy (1913) *Spanish Islam: A History of the Muslims in Spain* (translated by Francis Griffin Stokes from Dozy's original (1861) French *Histoire des Musulmans d'Espagne*, with consultation of the 1874 German version and the 1877 Spanish version) Chatto & Windus, London, page 133 https://books.google.com/books?id=AtQ7yAftTdQC&pg=PA133

[90] Levi-Provençal, (1950: p.48); Kennedy (1996: p.45).

[91] Franco Cardini, *Europe and Islam*, Wiley-Blackwell, 2001, p. 9

[92] Roger Collins, "The Arab Conquest of Spain, 710–797", pp. 113–140 & 168–182.

[93] Tertius Chandler. *Four Thousand Years of Urban Growth: An Historical Census* (1987), St. David's University Press (etext.org http://www.etext.org/Politics/World.Systems/datasets/citypop/civilizations/citypops_2000BC-1988AD).

[94] *Western Civilization: Ideas, Politics, and Society* https://books.google.com/books?id=kKGgoNo4un0C&pg=PA261&lpg=PA261, Marvin Perry, Myrna Chase, Margaret C. Jacob, James R. Jacob, 2008, 903 pages, p.261/262.

[95] Khaldun. The Muqaddimah

[96] Granada- The Last Refuge of Muslims in Spain http://www.muslimheritage.com/uploads/Granada.pdf by Salah Zaimeche

[97] L. P. Harvey: *Muslims in Spain, 1500 to 1614*. University of Chicago Press, 2008, , p. 1 ()

[98] *Vínculos Historia: The moriscos who remained. The permanence of Islamic origin population in Early Modern Spain: Kingdom of Granada, XVII-XVIII centuries* http://dialnet.unirioja.es/servlet/articulo?codigo=4040221 (In Spanish)

[99] Glick 1999, Chapter 5: Ethnic Relations.

[100] "The rate of conversion is slow until the tenth century (less than one-quarter of the eventual total number of converts had been converted); the explosive period coincides closely with the reign of 'Abd al-Rahmdn III (912–961); the process is completed (eighty percent converted) by around 1100. The curve, moreover, makes possible a reasonable estimate of the religious

distribution of the population. Assuming that there were seven million Hispano-Romans in the peninsula in 711 and that the numbers of this segment of the population remained level through the eleventh century (with population growth balancing out Christian migration to the north), then by 912 there would have been approximately 2.8 million indigenous Muslims (muwalladûn) plus Arabs and Berbers. At this point Christians still vastly outnumbered Muslims. By 1100, however, the number of indigenous Muslims would have risen to a majority of 5.6 million.", (Glick 1999, Chapter 1: At the crossroads of civilization)

[101] Wasserstein, 1995, p. 101.
[102] Jayyusi. The legacy of Muslim Spain
[103] Stavans, 2003, p. 10.
[104] Kraemer, 2005, pp. 10–13.
[105] O'Callaghan, 1975, p. 286.
[106] Roth, 1994, pp. 113–116.
[107] Frederick M. Schweitzer, Marvin Perry., *Anti-Semitism: myth and hate from antiquity to the present*, Palgrave Macmillan, 2002, , pp. 267–268.
[108] Granada http://jewishencyclopedia.com/view.jsp?artid=412&letter=G&search=Granada by Richard Gottheil, Meyer Kayserling, *Jewish Encyclopedia*. 1906 ed.
[109] Harzig, Hoerder and Shubert, 2003, p. 42.
[110] Islamic world. (2007). In Encyclopædia Britannica. Retrieved September 2, 2007, from Encyclopædia Britannica Online http://www.britannica.com/eb/article-26925.
[111] Frank and Leaman, 2003, pp. 137–138.
[112] Previte-Orton (1971), vol. 1, pg. 377
[113] http://libro.uca.edu/ics/emspain.htm
[114] http://libmma.contentdm.oclc.org/cdm/compoundobject/collection/p15324coll10/id/45966/rec/1
[115] http://www.degruyter.com/rs/261_264_DEU_h.htm
[116] http://www.bbc.co.uk/bbcfour/documentaries/features/islamic-history-europe.shtml
[117] https//web.archive.org
[118] https://web.archive.org/web/20051211030956/http://www.unesco.org/culture/al-andalus/html_eng/article.shtml
[119] http://libro.uca.edu/payne1/payne2.htm
[120] https://web.archive.org/web/20070512082946/http://www.paradoxplace.com/Photo%20Pages/Spain/Spain_History/Al-Andalus_Chronology.htm
[121] http://libro.uca.edu/martyrs/martyrs.htm
[122] https://web.archive.org/web/20091014132337/http://www.afropop.org/Alandalus/Alandalus.html
[123] https://web.archive.org/web/20110708141619/http://www.saudiaramcoworld.com/issue/199205/the.art.of.islamic.spain.htm
[124] http://www.islamicspain.tv
[125] http://www.gutenberg.org/ebooks/author/41035
[126] //tools.wmflabs.org/geohack/geohack.php?pagename=Al-Andalus&params=37_N_4_W_region:ES_type:country_scale:5000000
[127] //en.wikipedia.org/w/index.php?title=Template:History_of_the_Arab_League_member_states&action=edit
[128] Previte-Orton (1971), vol. 1, pg. 370
[129] Islam in Sicily http://images.alwialatas.multiply.com/attachment/0/RcF@1goKCrAAAB-to8o1/Islam%20in%20Sicily.doc?nmid=18936909 , by Alwi Alatas
[130] Archived link https://web.archive.org/web/20100821054137/http://www.cliohres.net/books/3/Dalli.pdf: *From Islam to Christianity: the Case of Sicily*, Charles Dalli, page 153. In *Religion, ritual and mythology : aspects of identity formation in Europe* / edited by Joaquim Carvalho, 2006, .
[131] Saracen Door and Battle of Palermo http://www.bestofsicily.com/mag/art139.htm
[132] Normans in Sicilian History http://www.bestofsicily.com/mag/art171.htm
[133] Roger II - Encyclopædia Britannica http://concise.britannica.com/ebc/article-9377080/Roger-II
[134] Tracing The Norman Rulers of Sicily https://query.nytimes.com/gst/fullpage.html?res=9B0DE1D61331F935A15757C0A961948260&sec=&spon=&pagewanted=2

[135] Charles Dalli, From Islam to Christianity: the Case of Sicily, p. 159 https://web.archive.org/web/20100821054137/http://www.cliohres.net/books/3/Dalli.pdf (archived link)
[136] Abulafia, The end of Muslim Sicily cit., p. 109
[137] Charles Dalli, *From Islam to Christianity: the Case of Sicily*, p. 159 https://web.archive.org/web/20100821054137/http://www.cliohres.net/books/3/Dalli.pdf (archived link)
[138] J. Johns, The Greek church and the conversion of Muslims in Norman Sicily?, "Byzantinische Forschungen", 21, 1995; for Greek Christianity in Sicily see also V. von Falkenhausen, "Il monachesimo greco in Sicilia", in C.D. Fonseca (ed.), *La Sicilia rupestre nel contesto delle civiltà mediterranee*, vol. 1, Lecce 1986.
[139] Charles Dalli, From Islam to Christianity: the Case of Sicily, p. 160 https://web.archive.org/web/20100821054137/http://www.cliohres.net/books/3/Dalli.pdf (archived link)
[140] Charles Dalli, From Islam to Christianity: the Case of Sicily, p. 160-161 https://web.archive.org/web/20100821054137/http://www.cliohres.net/books/3/Dalli.pdf (archived link)
[141] Charles Dalli, From Islam to Christianity: the Case of Sicily, p. 161 https://web.archive.org/web/20100821054137/http://www.cliohres.net/books/3/Dalli.pdf (archived link)
[142] A.Lowe: The Barrier and the bridge, op cit;p.92.
[143] Saracen Archers in Southern Italy http://www.deremilitari.org/resources/articles/saracen_archers.htm
[144] http://www.historyfiles.co.uk/KingListsEurope/ItalySicily.htm
[145] https://web.archive.org/web/20100616060825/http://imamreza.net/eng/imamreza.php?id=630
[146] Lebedel, p.109
[147] Lebedel, p.113
[148] Lewis, p.148
[149] Lebedel, p.109–111
[150] "Avicenna", Lenn Evan Goodman, 2006, p. 209
[151] Corbin, History of Islamic Philosophy (1993), p.174
[152]
[153] "Inventions et decouvertes au Moyen-Age", Samuel Sadaune, p.112
[154] According to Margaret Smith (1944), "There can be no doubt that Ghazali's works would be among the first to attract the attention of these European scholars" and "The greatest of these Christian writers who was influenced by Al-Ghazali was St. Thomas Aquinas (1225–1274), who made a study of the Islamic writers and admitted his indebtedness to them. He studied at the University of Naples where the influence of Islamic literature and culture was predominant at the time." Margaret Smith, *Al-Ghazali: The Mystic* (London 1944)
[155] Fielding H. Garrison, *An Introduction to the History of Medicine: with Medical Chronology, Suggestions for Study and Biblographic Data*, p. 86
[156] Lebedel, p.111
[157] Lebedel, p.112
[158] C. Burnett, "Arabic-Latin Translation Program in Toledo", p. 255.
[159] C. H. Haskins, *Studies in the History of Mediaeval Science*, pp.3-4
[160] R. W. Southern, *The Making of the Middle Ages*, p.65
[161] For a list of Gerard of Cremona's translations see: Edward Grant (1974) *A Source Book in Medieval Science*, (Cambridge: Harvard Univ. Pr.), pp. 35–38 or Charles Burnett, "The Coherence of the Arabic-Latin Translation Program in Toledo in the Twelfth Century," *Science in Context*, 14 (2001): at 249–288, at pp. 275–281.
[162] D. Campbell, *Arabian Medicine and Its Influence on the Middle Ages*, p. 6.
[163] Eric John Holmyard, *Alchemy*, p.106
[164] Eric John Holmyard, *Alchemy*, p.109
[165] A few of the Latin works are now attributed to a Pseudo-Geber, as although attributed to "Geber", they have no identified Arabic source and appear to have been composed in Latin in the 13th century.<ref>Eric John Holmyard, *Alchemy*, pp.134-135
[166] G. G. Joseph, *The Crest of the Peacock*, p. 306
[167] David Pingree (1964), "Gregory Chioniades and Palaeologan Astronomy", *Dumbarton Oaks Papers* **18**, p. 135–160.
[168]

[169] H. Salih, M. Al-Amri, M. El Gomati (2005). " The Miracle of Light http://unesdoc.unesco.org/images/0014/001412/141236E.pdf", *A World of Science* **3** (3), UNESCO

[170] Richard Powers (University of Illinois), Best Idea; Eyes Wide Open http://online.physics.uiuc.edu/courses/phys199epp/fall06/Powers-NYTimes.pdf , *New York Times*, April 18, 1999.

[171] Moody, Ernest A. (1951), "Galileo and Avempace: The Dynamics of the Leaning Tower Experiment (I)", *Journal of the History of Ideas* **12** (2): 163–193

[172] Charles Burnett, ed. *Adelard of Bath, Conversations with His Nephew*, (Cambridge: Cambridge University Press, 1999), p. xi.

[173]

[174] "Inventions et decouvertes au Moyen-Age", Samuel Sadaune, p.44

[175] National Library of Medicine digital archives

[176] David W. Tschanz, MSPH, PhD (August 2003). "Arab Roots of European Medicine", *Heart Views* **4** (2).

[177] D. Campbell, *Arabian Medicine and Its Influence on the Middle Ages*, p. 3.

[178] Albucasis http://www.sciencemuseum.org.uk/broughttolife/people/albucasis.aspx Science museum on Albucasis

[179] M.-T. d'Alverny, "Translations and Translators," pp. 444–446, 451

[180] M.-T. d'Alverny, "Translations and Translators," pp. 429, 455

[181] "Les Normans en Sicile"

[182] Roux, p. 47

[183] Mack, 3-8, and throughout

[184] Mack, p.65–66

[185] Mack, p.51

[186] Mack, p.52, p.69

[187] "Perhaps they marked the imagery of a universal faith, an artistic intention consistent with the Church's contemporary international program." Mack, p.69

[188] M. Guettat (1980), *La Musique classique du Maghreb* (Paris: Sindbad).

[189] "Troubadour", *Grove Dictionary of Music and Musicians*, edited by Stanley Sadie, Macmillan Press Ltd., London

[190] David A. King (2002). "A Vetustissimus Arabic Text on the Quadrans Vetus", *Journal for the History of Astronomy* **33**, p. 237–255 [237–238].

[191] The Saphea Arzachelis http://astrolabes.org/saphea.htm , astrolabes.org

[192] Ahmad Y Hassan, Transfer Of Islamic Technology To The West, Part II: Transmission Of Islamic Engineering http://www.history-science-technology.com/Articles/articles%2071.htm , *History of Science and Technology in Islam*

[193] "Studies in Medieval Islamic Technology: From Philo to Al-Jazari - From Alexandria to Diya Bakr", Donald Routledge Hill and David A. King, p.23, 1998,

[194]

[195] Michael Decker: "Plants and Progress: Rethinking the Islamic Agricultural Revolution", Journal of World History, Vol. 20, No. 2 (2009), pp. 187-206

[196] "The Sugar Cane Industry: An Historical Geography from Its Origins to 1914 (1989)", pp.34-34, JH Galloway,

[197] Ahmad Y Hassan, Transfer Of Islamic Technology To The West, Part 1: Avenues Of Technology Transfer http://www.history-science-technology.com/Articles/articles%207.htm

[198] Adam Lucas (2006), *Wind, Water, Work: Ancient and Medieval Milling Technology*, p. 10 & 65, BRILL, .

[199] Ahmad Y Hassan. The Origin of the Suction Pump http://www.history-science-technology.com/Notes/Notes%202.htm .

[200] Quoted in "The Sugar Cane Industry: An Historical Geography from Its Origins to 1914", JH Galloway, p. 27

[201] Adam Robert Lucas (2005), "Industrial Milling in the Ancient and Medieval Worlds: A Survey of the Evidence for an Industrial Revolution in Medieval Europe", *Technology and Culture* **46** (1), pp. 1–30.

[202] British Museum

[203] Blanchard, Ian *Mining, Metallurgy and Minting in the Middle Ages* Franz Steiner Verlag, 2001 https://books.google.com/books?id=Zo2UVs_Sr68C&pg=PA196&dq=tari+coins, p.196

[204] British Museum, Islamic Art room
[205] Cardini, Franco *Europe and Islam* Blackwell Publishing, 2001 https://books.google.com/books?id=pePPvGkGZDQC&pg=PA26&dq=kharruba+coin&lr=, p.26
[206] Grierson, Philip *Medieval European Coinage* Cambridge University Press, 1998. https://books.google.com/books?id=jgSNmsXG1jwC&pg=PA63&dq=kharruba+coin#PPA3,M1, p.3
[207] Janet Abu-Lughod *Before European Hegemony, The World System A.D. 1250–1350*, Oxford University Press, p.15
[208] I. Heullant-Donat and M.-A. Polo de Beaulieu, "Histoire d'une traduction," in *Le Livre de l'échelle de Mahomet*, Latin edition and French translation by Gisèle Besson and Michèle Brossard-Dandré, Collection *Lettres Gothiques*, Le Livre de Poche, 1991, p. 22 with note 37.
[209] //doi.org/10.2307/839667
[210] //www.jstor.org/stable/839667
[211] //www.worldcat.org/oclc/220811631
[212] //www.worldcat.org/oclc/181885553
[213] //www.worldcat.org/oclc/36229500
[214] https//books.google.com
[215] https://plato.stanford.edu/entries/arabic-islamic-influence/
[216] https://web.archive.org/web/20110727013452/http://www.lssu.edu/faculty/jswedene/FULBRIGHT_FILES/Islamic%20Contributions%20to%20the%20West.doc
[217] http://www.aina.org/books/hgsptta.htm
[218] http://bahai-library.com/cobb_islamic_contributions_civilization
[219] James Chamber, *The Devil's Horsemen: The Mongol Invasion of Europe*, (Edison: Castle Books, 2003), page 33.
[220] Jane I. Smith. "Islam and Christendom," in *The Oxford History of Islam*. Edited by John L. Esposito. *Oxford Islamic Studies Online*. http://www.oxfordislamicstudies.com/article. (accessed January 29, 2008), page 1.
[221] "Andalusia." The Islamic World: Past and Present. Edited by John L. Esposito. Oxford Islamic Studies Online, http://www.oxfordislamicstudies.com/article (accessed February 2, 2008).
[222] "Granada." The Oxford Dictionary of Islam. Edited by John L. Esposito. Oxford Islamic Studies Online, http://www.oxfordislamicstudies.com/article (accessed February 2, 2008).
[223] "Andalusia."
[224] David Nicole, El Cid and the Reconquista: 1050-1492, (Great Britain: Osprey Publishing Limited, 1988), page 8.
[225] David Nicole, page 39.
[226] "Granada."
[227] "Alhambra." The Oxford Dictionary of Islam. Edited by John L. Esposito. Oxford Islamic Studies Online, http://www.oxfordislamicstudies.com/article (accessed February 2, 2008).
[228] [/religion/religions/islam/history/uk_1.shtml BBC]
[229] Voyager's Tales, 3, The voyage made to Tripolis in Barbary,1584 http://historicaltextarchive.com/books.php?op=viewbook&bookid=51&cid=3, Richard Haklyut
[230] Rees Davies, British Slaves on the Barbary Coast http://www.bbc.co.uk/history/british/empire_seapower/white_slaves_01.shtml, BBC, 1 July 2003
[231] History of Lundy http://www.lundyisland.co.uk/history.htm
[232] Everett Jenkins, Jr., the Muslim Diaspora: a Comprehensive Reference to the Spread of Islam in Asia, Africa, Europe, and the Americas. (Jefferson, NC: McFarland and Company, Inc., 2000), 2:7.
[233] Isa Blumi. "Kosovo." The Oxford Encyclopedia of the Islamic World. Edited by John L. Esposito. Oxford Islamic Studies Online. http://www.oxfordislamicstudies.com/article. (accessed January 29, 2008)
[234] P.S. Konningsveld, P.S., page15.
[235] P.S. Konningsveld, page16.
[236] P.S. Konningsveld, page10.
[237] P.S. Konningsveld, page6.
[238] Ecouen Museum exhibit
[239] *Whose Science is Arabic Science in Renaissance Europe?* by George Saliba Columbia University http://www.columbia.edu/~gas1/project/visions/case1/sci.4.html

[240] Arthur Augustus Tilley, *The Literature of the French Renaissance*, p. 87 https://books.google.com/books?id=UEzBBwwzjXkC&pg=PA87

[241] *The Penny cyclopædia of the Society for the Diffusion of Useful Knowledge* p.418 https://books.google.com/books?id=7KsrAAAAYAAJ&pg=PA418

[242] Jon Mcginnis, *Classical Arabic Philosophy: An Anthology of Sources*, p. 284, Hackett Publishing Company, .

[243] Samar Attar, *The Vital Roots of European Enlightenment: Ibn Tufayl's Influence on Modern Western Thought*, Lexington Books, .http://bookshop.blackwell.co.uk/jsp/id/The_Vital_Roots_of_European_Enlightenment/9780739119891

[244] Nawal Muhammad Hassan (1980), *Hayy bin Yaqzan and Robinson Crusoe: A study of an early Arabic impact on English literature*, Al-Rashid House for Publication.

[245] Cyril Glasse (2001), *New Encyclopedia of Islam*, p. 202, Rowman Altamira, .

[246] Amber Haque (2004), "Psychology from Islamic Perspective: Contributions of Early Muslim Scholars and Challenges to Contemporary Muslim Psychologists", *Journal of Religion and Health* **43** (4): 357-377 [369].

[247] Martin Wainwright, Desert island scripts http://books.guardian.co.uk/review/story/0,12084,918454,00.html, *The Guardian*, 22 March 2003.

[248] Professor Nabil Matar (April 2004), *Shakespeare and the Elizabethan Stage Moor*, Sam Wanamaker Fellowship Lecture, Shakespeare's Globe Theatre (cf. Mayor of London (2006), Muslims in London http://www.london.gov.uk/gla/publications/equalities/muslims-in-london.pdf, pp. 14-15, Greater London Authority)

[249] G. A. Russell, The 'Arabick' Interest of the Natural Philosophers in Seventeenth-century England, BRILL, 1994, , p. 162

[250] Nabil I. Matar, "Renaissance England and the Turban," Images of the Other: Europe and the Muslim World Before 1700 Ed. David Blanks, (Cairo: Cairo Press, 1997).

[251] Nabil I. Matar, "Renaissance England and the Turban."

[252] Nabil Matar, "The Representation of Muslim Women in Renaissance England," page 51.

[253] Nabil Matar, "The Representation of Muslim Women in Renaissance England," page 52.

[254] Nabil Matar, "The Representation of Muslim Women in Renaissance England," page 61.

[255] Nabil Matar, "The Representation of Muslim Women in Renaissance England," page 53 and 54.

[256] Nabil Matar, "The Representation of Muslim Women in Renaissance England," page 60.

Article Sources and Contributors

The sources listed for each article provide more detailed licensing information including the copyright status, the copyright owner, and the license conditions.

Islam in Europe *Source*: https://en.wikipedia.org/w/index.php?oldid=853555866 *License*: Creative Commons Attribution-Share Alike 3.0 *Contributors*: 2minty, 78.26, 8ankitj, AadaamS, Abhi.raya, Adamgerber80, Adoring nanny, Al-Andalusi, Alessandro57, Alexander Domanda, Alghenius, Ali-al-Bakuvi, Alpha3031, Alumnum, AndyTheGrump, Arjayay, Arsi786, Art LaPella, AvatarofPride, Bender235, Beyond My Ken, Bgwhite, Blackguard SF, Bobfrombrockley, Bolialia, BoogaLouie, Britfan97, Bungler91, Caitlin030, Campista1891, CataracticPlanets, Catlemur, Chongkian, ClueBot NG, DanielDanielDaniel, Darkness Shines, Dr Gangrene, Dthomsen8, Editor2020, Elinruby, Emir of Wikipedia, Euripides ψ, Factsoverfeelings, Fahrenheit666, Fandecaisses, Finlandestonia, FreeatlastChitchat, Gabru Beclean, GjonMarkuu, GreenC, Grizlyy, Guy Macon, Heilhixtler1933, IRISZOOM, Ibadibam, Imnangel4u2c, Inactive user 20171, Iselilja, JStressman, Jackfork, Jarble, Jason from nyc, Jeppiz, Jim1138, JimRenge, Jobas, John of Reading, Kansas Bear, Kevjassintkevin, Khirurg, Kulmanseidl, Lappspira, LeRoiDesRois, Llaanngg, Local hero, LouisAragon, M2545, MHSLO, Marxistfounder, Melik, Memedhe, MenenbergLover, Michael G. Lind, Mikeblas, Milktaco, Mingling2, Mishaelyabes, MusenInvincible, Narky Blert, NawlinWiki, NebY, NeroN BG, Niceguyedc, Nillurcheier, Non-dropframe, Pailsdell, Peregrine981, Ponyo, Quackriot, Resnjari, Rich Farmbrough, Rivertorch, Rob78789, Rolf-Peter Wille, Rong Qiqi, RutiliusClaudiusNamatianus, Sdino, Shellwood, SilentResident, Sjö, Squip592, Sro23, Stanley89eightnine, Sukesi, Sztyepan, Tensor-product, The Almighty Drill, ThisIsAgain32, Tiiliskivi, Tobby72, Tolea93, Tomwalker89, Trappist the monk, Visite fortuitement prolongée, Wbm1058, Wwikix, Zoupan, 144 anonymous edits 1

Moors *Source*: https://en.wikipedia.org/w/index.php?oldid=853465139 *License*: Creative Commons Attribution-Share Alike 3.0 *Contributors*: Abune, Ad Orientem, Asherblake, Asmodim, Atlas, BD2412, Barbe Queen, Barek, BrugesFR, CambridgeBayWeather, ChrisTakey, CliffordPereira, Clue-Bot NG, CoolieCoolster, Cwiley76, D A R C 12345, DJAustin, Dachicabonita, Daniel Power of God, DerekHistorian, Diannaa, Dimadick, Divermanh AU, Doug Weller, Drmies, EdJohnston, Emerarudo, Gatemansgc, Gilliam, HaEr48, Hairy Dude, Holdoffhunger, Jarble, Javert2113, JayLady, John, KangJa-mal, Kannelambre, Kansas Bear, Katangais, Kintetsubuffalo, Laszlo Panaflex, LibertyEd1850, Loaka1, M.Bitton, Mandruss, Maproom, Marcocapelle, Mario A. Castro-Rojas, Maximajorian Viridio, Name goes here, Ogress, One Of Seven Billion, Oshwah, Pinkbeast, Rich Farmbrough, RickinBaltimore, Rodw, Roger 8 Roger, Samf4u, SarekOfVulcan, Shellwood, Shityymcassentire, Soupforone, Sphilbrick, Supergirl30353035, TAnthony, Tarook97, Ticyo, Tobby72, Tom.Reding, Tom112233, Velteau, Widr, Yamaguchi先生, ملاعم نب دمحم, سمّم, 102 anonymous edits 21

Al-Andalus *Source*: https://en.wikipedia.org/w/index.php?oldid=853295662 *License*: Creative Commons Attribution-Share Alike 3.0 *Contributors*: Agricolae, Abecht, Alhaqiba, Asqueladd, Bender235, Berthold Werner, BrugesFR, Carlstak, Chewings72, Chiswick Chap, ClueBot NG, CommonsDelinker, CounterTime, Crackedkettle, DA1, DASDBILL2, Dariovitori, Dayvenkirq, Dbachmann, Dcirovic, Deisenbe, Dimadick, Dorpater, Doug Weller, Eperoton, Esrever, Ewen, Favonian, Fofo235, Gatemansgc, Gauhar2806, GreenMeansGo, Grenzer22, HaEr48, Iacobus, Inactive user 20171, JesseRafe, Jessicapierce, John, John of Reading, Jotamar, Kaitlynn80, Kansas Bear, Kazvorpal, Kleuske, Kmhkmh, Knowledgge, Kotabatubara, Laszlo Panaflex, Liiiii, Lindasun123, Loaka1, Loginnigol, Look2See1, LuzoGraal, Marcocapelle, Marek69, Marianna251, MonsterHunter32, MoorishAmir, Mubeda, Muhammed al ahazred, NewEnglandYankee, Olea, Optakeover, Oshwah, Pinkbeast, Pro gǜvo, Pórokhov, Quisqualis, Rich Farmbrough, Rrburke, Rwenonah, Salaheldin Mohamed Ali, Sangdeboeuf, Serols, Siddiqsazzad001, Simon Peter Hughes, Sirlanz, Srnec, Swazzo, Tajotep, Taosizhehit, Tarook97, The Almighty Drill, Thelastau-roch, Tiago Wilcke, Torvalu4, Tropicalkitty, Vejlefjord, Veritas2016, Vermont, Vihelik, Vvven, Wiki Wikardo, XPTO, 96 anonymous edits 41

Emirate of Sicily *Source*: https://en.wikipedia.org/w/index.php?oldid=853180324 *License*: Creative Commons Attribution-Share Alike 3.0 *Contributors*: Actio, Againme, Agilulf2007, AjaxSmack, Alamanin, Aldis90, Alessandro57, Alexander Domanda, Angusmclellan, Art LaPella, Ashrf1979, At-tilios, Awewe, Azure94, BD2412, Badurns, Baking Soda, CardinalDan, Cataloprapher, Civa61, Clean Copy, Cplakidas, Dbachmann, Dentren, Dimadick, DonCalo, DrRC, Drmies, Edwoed, Elmer Clark, ErikWarmelink, Famartin, Favenatic london, Felix Folio Secundus, Freenau, Future Perfect at Sunrise, GCarty, General Grievous, Generic User, Gennarous, Gob Lofa, Griffindd, Gun Powder Ma, Hmains, Hon-3s-T, Ian Spackman, Ignoranteconomist, Ima-reaver, Indiasummer95, Iryna Harpy, Jagged 85, JamesBWatson, Jeff3000, Jeffmatt, Jessicapierce, Kafka Liz, Kansas Bear, Khestwol, Kostja, Krenakarore, Ktr101, Liberal Humanist, Llywrch, LoneWolf1992, Lylefor, MacsBug, Maltesemizzi, MarcusVestu, Maurice Carbonaro, Member, Menah the Great, Metron, Michael!, Mimihitam, Moonriddengirl, Mountolive, MuhammadBinTimothy, MusenInvincible, Mxcatania, Nabbateus, Nakhoda84, Neutrality, Niceguyedc, Ninly, Omaronly, PMLawrence, Pavel Vozenilek, Penguins Are Animals 5327, Pippu d'Angelo, Polaron, Pol984, R'n'B, Rich Farm-brough, Ricky81682, Rjwilmsi, Robertgreer, Sadistik, Scythian1, SeNeKa, Senjuto, Serban Maron, Sicilianu101, Spettro9, Spiff~enwiki, Spirtzis, Steven J. Anderson, SufianBak, SugnuSicilianu, Tarook97, The Almighty Drill, The Anomebot2, The Banner, The Sage of Stamford, The White Lion, TheUnder-dark, Theodorevp, Tommylotto, Trey Kincaid, Vaselineeeeeeee, Vegaswikian, Waterloo1974, WereSpielChequers, Wgolf, WhisperToMe, Woohookitty, ÄDA - DÄP, תי, 2 136 anonymous edits 65

Islamic world contributions to Medieval Europe *Source*: https://en.wikipedia.org/w/index.php?oldid=839236907 *License*: Creative Commons Attribution-Share Alike 3.0 *Contributors*: AkramBinWallid, Al-Andalusi, AlexanderVanLoon, Alexis Ivanov, Altetendekrabbe, Amandajm, Archeologo, AsceticRose, Aymatth2, BD2412, Bender235, Bentogoa, Big iron, Bloodofox, Br3npon, CAPTAIN RAJU, Chiswick Chap, Chris the speller, Citation bot 1, ClueBot NG, ColRad85, Cyclopedion, David.moreno72, Dbachmann, Dialectric, Discospinster, Donner60, Doug Weller, Eliassagar, Eumolpo, Excirial, Eyesnore, EzraEn, FoCuSandLeArN, FriyMan, Gilliam, Gun Powder Ma, Headbomb, HelloAnnyong, Hmains, Hugo999, JI079s, Jamietw, Jamool66, Jorgenev, Jupitus Smart, Kansas Bear, Kelbin12, Khazar2, LilHelpa, Lizard146, Lololololol fail, Look2See1, M Todorovic, Madreterra, Mandarax, Mate-rialscientist, MelbourneStar, Menenberg+Bacon=Baconberg, Merlinme, Michael Chidester, Mughal Lohar, NPrice, Niceguyedc, Nono64, Oshwah, PBS-AWB, PKT, PenguinHistory, Pinethicket, Rjwilmsi, SamuelTheGhost, Saralie, SchreiberBike, Sebastianmaali, SheriffIsInTown, Soldier of the Empire, Sunrise, Swingoswingo, Tarook97, Tassedethe, Trappist the monk, Tu74, Turjan, Vermont, Vice regent, WOSlinker, Widr, William M. Connolley, Wood-lot, Woohookitty, Yosri, ZxxZxxZ, 106 anonymous edits 76

Reception of Islam in Early Modern Europe *Source*: https://en.wikipedia.org/w/index.php?oldid=799248773 *License*: Creative Commons Attribution-Share Alike 3.0 *Contributors*: Attilios, Auntof6, Big iron, Biruitorul, BjörnEF, Chicbyaccident, ClueBot NG, CommonsDelinker, DGG, Dbachmann, Dthomsen8, Edward, Ev, Fayenatic london, Gatoclass, GoingBatty, Goustien, Guoguo12, Hmains, I dream of horses, Iraka verona, Jack Greenmaven, Jagged 85, Johnbod, Marcosoldfox, Marek69, Mogism, Moonraker, Oreo Priest, PFHLai, Per Honor et Gloria, Prhartcom, R'n'B, Robofish, Ronhjones, Sp-141, Squids and Chips, Swingoswingo, Takabeg, ThatPeskyCommoner, The Emperor's New Spy, Thirdright, Wiae, 13 anonymous edits 99

Image Sources, Licenses and Contributors

The sources listed for each image provide more detailed licensing information including the copyright status, the copyright owner, and the license conditions.

Figure 1 *Source:* https://en.wikipedia.org/w/index.php?title=File:Islam_in_Europe-2010.svg *License:* Creative Commons Attribution-Sharealike 3.0 *Contributors:* File:Blank map of Europe - Atelier graphique colors with Kosovo.svg: MichaelBueker and others File:Islam in Europe-2.png 2

Figure 2 *Source:* https://en.wikipedia.org/w/index.php?title=File:Jaume_I,_Cantigas_de_Santa_Maria,_s.XIII.jpg *License:* Public Domain *Contributors:* Alphonse X of Castile 3

Figure 3 *Source:* https://en.wikipedia.org/w/index.php?title=File:Araz.jpg *License:* GNU Free Documentation License *Contributors:* Alex Tora, Czarnyowiec, DarwIn, Gustavo Szwedowski de Korwin, Ilyaroz, Kilom691, MGA73bot2, Massimop, VIGNERON, Иван Дулин 4

Figure 4 *Source:* https://en.wikipedia.org/w/index.php?title=File:Grande_Mosquée_de_Paris.JPG *License:* Creative Commons Attribution-Share Alike *Contributors:* LPLT 5

Figure 5 *Source:* https://en.wikipedia.org/w/index.php?title=File:Mošeja-Log_pod_Mangartom4.jpg *License:* Public Domain *Contributors:* Eleassar, Janezdrilc, Yerpo 6

Figure 6 *Source:* https://en.wikipedia.org/w/index.php?title=File:Szigetvar_1566.jpg *License:* Public Domain *Contributors:* Lokman 7

Figure 7 *Source:* https://en.wikipedia.org/w/index.php?title=File:Szulejmán_a_sátrában_Buda_alatt_(1529).JPG *License:* Public Domain *Contributors:* Doncsecz, Hohum, Pe-Jo, Shakko, ZxxZxxZ 8

Figure 8 *Source:* https//en.wikipedia.org *License:* Public Domain *Contributors:* Chevalier Auguste de Henikstein 8

Figure 9 *Source:* https://en.wikipedia.org/w/index.php?title=File:Bazar_of_Athens.jpg *License:* Public Domain *Contributors:* Andrew Dalby, Badseed, BotMultichill, BotMultichillT, BronHiggs, Cplakidas, Jonathan Groß, Wieralee 9

Figure 10 *Source:* https://en.wikipedia.org/w/index.php?title=File:Janissary_Recruitment_in_the_Balkans-Suleymanname.jpg *Contributors:* Ali Amir Beg (fl. 1558) 10

Figure 11 *Source:* https://en.wikipedia.org/w/index.php?title=File:Sultan_Murat_Fatih_mosque,_Prishtina_Kosovo.JPG *Contributors:* User:Aljabakphoto 12

Figure 12 *Source:* https://en.wikipedia.org/w/index.php?title=File:IslamInEurope.png *License:* GNU Free Documentation License *Contributors:* User:Scooter20 12

Figure 13 *Source:* https://en.wikipedia.org/w/index.php?title=File:Muslim_pop_Euro.JPG *License:* Creative Commons Zero *Contributors:* Vice regent 13

Image *Source:* https://en.wikipedia.org/w/index.php?title=File:Flag_of_Albania.svg *License:* Public Domain *Contributors:* User:Dbenbenn ... 15

Image *Source:* https://en.wikipedia.org/w/index.php?title=File:Flag_of_Andorra.svg *License:* Public Domain *Contributors:* Anime Addict AA, Avala, Benzoyl, Cathy Richards, Cycn, Dbenbenn, Denelson83, Duduziq, Enbéká, Froztbyte, Fry1989, George McFinnigan, HansenBCN, Hedwig in Washington, HoheHoffnungen, Homo lupus, Ilfga, Juetho, Kanonkas, Klemen Kocjancic, LuCKY, MAXXX-309, Manvydasz, Mattes, Neq00, Patricia.fidi, Prev, Sarang, SiBr4, Smaug the Golden, Suisui, TFerenczy, Vzb83~commonswiki, XJMsa, Zscout370, 2 anonymous edits 15

Image *Source:* https://en.wikipedia.org/w/index.php?title=File:Flag_of_Austria.svg *License:* Public Domain *Contributors:* User:SKopp 15

Image *Source:* https://en.wikipedia.org/w/index.php?title=File:Flag_of_Belarus.svg *License:* Public Domain *Contributors:* Zscout370 15

Image *Source:* https://en.wikipedia.org/w/index.php?title=File:Flag_of_Belgium_(civil).svg *License:* Public Domain *Contributors:* Allforrous, Andres gb.ldc, Bean49, Cathy Richards, David Descamps, Dbenbenn, Denelson83, Evanc0912, FreshCorp619, Fry1989, Gabriel trzy, Howcome, IvanOS, Jdx, Mimich, Ms2ger, Nightstallion, Oreo Priest, Pitke, Ricordisamoa, Rocket000, Rodejong, Sarang, SiBr4, Sir Iain, ThomasPusch, Warddr, Zscout370, ייהלייוושמר, 15 anonymous edits 15

Image *Source:* https://en.wikipedia.org/w/index.php?title=File:Flag_of_Bosnia_and_Herzegovina.svg *License:* Public Domain *Contributors:* Kseferovic 15

Image *Source:* https://en.wikipedia.org/w/index.php?title=File:Flag_of_Bulgaria.svg *License:* Public Domain *Contributors:* SKopp 15

Image *Source:* https://en.wikipedia.org/w/index.php?title=File:Flag_of_Croatia.svg *License:* Public Domain *Contributors:* Nightstallion, Elephantus, Neoneo13, Denelson83, Rainman, R-41, Minestrone, Lupo, Zscout370, MaGa (based on Decision of 15

Image *Source:* https://en.wikipedia.org/w/index.php?title=File:Flag_of_Cyprus.svg *License:* Public Domain *Contributors:* User:Vzb83 15

Image *Source:* https://en.wikipedia.org/w/index.php?title=File:Flag_of_the_Czech_Republic.svg *License:* Public Domain *Contributors:* -xfi-, Alkari, Andres gb.ldc, AwOc, Benzoyl, Bjankuloski06en, C41n, Cycn, Denelson83, Denniss, Dzordzm, EZBELLA, Er Komandante, Fedor204, Fibonacci, FreshCorp619, Fry1989, Future Perfect at Sunrise, Gumruch, Homo lupus, JuTa, Klemen Kocjancic, Leyo, Li-sung, MAXXX-309, Madden, Miraceti, NeverDoING, Nightstallion, Pfctdayelise, Phlegmatic, Pseudomoi, Pumbaa80, Ratatosk, Ricordisamoa, Saibo, Sangjinhwa, Sarang, Shybird, SiBr4, Stephanie~commonswiki, V-ball, Wiki-vr, علی المزارقه, 43 anonymous edits 15

Image *Source:* https://en.wikipedia.org/w/index.php?title=File:Flag_of_Denmark.svg *License:* Public Domain *Contributors:* Madden 15

Image *Source:* https://en.wikipedia.org/w/index.php?title=File:Flag_of_Estonia.svg *License:* Public Domain *Contributors:* Originally drawn by User:SKopp. Blue colour changed by User:PeepP to match the image at 15

Image *Source:* https://en.wikipedia.org/w/index.php?title=File:Flag_of_the_Faroe_Islands.svg *License:* Public Domain *Contributors:* User:IceKarma 15

Image *Source:* https://en.wikipedia.org/w/index.php?title=File:Flag_of_Finland.svg *License:* Public Domain *Contributors:* SVG drawn by Sebastian Koppehel 15

Image *Source:* https://en.wikipedia.org/w/index.php?title=File:Flag_of_France.svg *License:* Public Domain *Contributors:* Anomie, Fastily, Jo-Jo Eumerus 15

Image *Source:* https://en.wikipedia.org/w/index.php?title=File:Flag_of_Germany.svg *License:* Public Domain *Contributors:* Anomie, Jo-Jo Eumerus 15

Image *Source:* https://en.wikipedia.org/w/index.php?title=File:Flag_of_Greece.svg *License:* Public Domain *Contributors:* (of code) cs:User:-xfi-(talk) 15

Image *Source:* https://en.wikipedia.org/w/index.php?title=File:Flag_of_Hungary.svg *License:* Public Domain *Contributors:* SKopp 15

Image *Source:* https://en.wikipedia.org/w/index.php?title=File:Flag_of_Iceland.svg *License:* Public Domain *Contributors:* ALE!, ArniDagur, Benzoyl, Cathy Richards, Duduziq, Enbéká, F l a n k e r, F. F. Fjodor, Fry1989, GeMet, GoldenRainbow, Homo lupus, Iketsi, IvanOS, Jarekt, Juetho, Klemen Kocjancic, Liambaker98, Lirion, MAXXX-309, Magasjukur2, Mattes, Peeperman, RainbowSilver2ndBackup, S.Örvarr.S, Sarang, SiBr4, Superzerocool, ThomasPusch, Yarl, Zscout370, Ævar Arnfjörð Bjarmason, 8 anonymous edits 15

Image *Source:* https://en.wikipedia.org/w/index.php?title=File:Flag_of_Ireland.svg *License:* Public Domain *Contributors:* User:SKopp 15

Image *Source:* https://en.wikipedia.org/w/index.php?title=File:Flag_of_Italy.svg *License:* Public Domain *Contributors:* Anomie, Jo-Jo Eumerus 15

Image *Source:* https://en.wikipedia.org/w/index.php?title=File:Flag_of_Kosovo.svg *License:* Public Domain *Contributors:* Cradel (current version), earlier version by Ningyou 16

Image *Source:* https://en.wikipedia.org/w/index.php?title=File:Flag_of_Latvia.svg *License:* Public Domain *Contributors:* Anime Addict AA, Cathy Richards, Ciervo258, Common Good, Cycn, Dark Eagle, David1010, Edgars2007, Editor at Large, Fred J, Fry1989, Homo lupus, IvanOS, Kalnroze, Klemen Kocjancic, Ludger1961, MAXXX-309, Mattes, Ninane, OAlexander~commonswiki, RainbowSilver2ndBackup, Renessaince, Ricordisamoa, Rocket000, SKopp, Sarang, TFerenczy, V. Turchaninov, Wester, Zscout370, 12 anonymous edits 16

Image *Source:* https://en.wikipedia.org/w/index.php?title=File:Flag_of_Liechtenstein.svg *License:* Public Domain *Contributors:* User:Mnmazur 16

Image *Source:* https://en.wikipedia.org/w/index.php?title=File:Flag_of_Lithuania.svg *License:* Public Domain *Contributors:* Agente Rolf, CemDemirkartal, CrimsonViking, David1010, Fred J, Fry1989, GiW, Homo lupus, IvanOS, Juetho, Klemen Kocjancic, Ludger1961, Madden, Matasg, Nightstallion, Ninane, Ricordisamoa, Rodejong, SKopp, Sarang, TFerenczy, Telman Masliukou, ThomasPusch, Wizardist, Zscout370, Zzyzx11, חיים 7, 13 anonymous edits 16

Image *Source:* https://en.wikipedia.org/w/index.php?title=File:Flag_of_Luxembourg.svg *License:* Public Domain *Contributors:* User:SKopp .. 16

Image *Source:* https://en.wikipedia.org/w/index.php?title=File:Flag_of_Macedonia.svg *License:* Public Domain *Contributors:* User:Gabbe, User:SKopp 16

Image *Source:* https://en.wikipedia.org/w/index.php?title=File:Flag_of_Malta.svg *License:* Public Domain *Contributors:* Alkari, Allforrous, Cathy Richards, Cycn, File Upload Bot (Magnus Manske), Fry1989, Gabbe, GoldenRainbow, Hedwig in Washington, Herbythyme, Homo lupus, Klemen Kocjancic, Liftarn, Mattes, Meno25, Nightstallion, Peeperman, Prev, Pumbaa80, Ratatosk, Raymond1922A, Rodejong, Sangjinhwa, SiBr4, Xwejnusgozo, Yiyi, Zscout370, 7 anonymous edits 16

Image *Source:* https://en.wikipedia.org/w/index.php?title=File:Flag_of_Moldova.svg *License:* Public Domain *Contributors:* User:Nameneko .. 16

Image *Source:* https://en.wikipedia.org/w/index.php?title=File:Flag_of_Monaco.svg *License:* Public Domain *Contributors:* User:SKopp 16

Image *Source:* https://en.wikipedia.org/w/index.php?title=File:Flag_of_Montenegro.svg *Contributors:* B1mbo, Froztbyte 16

Image *Source:* https://en.wikipedia.org/w/index.php?title=File:Flag_of_the_Netherlands.svg *License:* Public Domain *Contributors:* Zscout370 16

Image *Source:* https://en.wikipedia.org/w/index.php?title=File:Flag_of_Norway.svg *License:* Public Domain *Contributors:* Dbenbenn 16

Image Source: https://en.wikipedia.org/w/index.php?title=File:Flag_of_Poland.svg License: Public Domain Contributors: Anomie, Jo-Jo Eumerus, Mifter ... 16
Image Source: https://en.wikipedia.org/w/index.php?title=File:Flag_of_Portugal.svg License: Public Domain Contributors: Columbano Bordalo Pinheiro (1910; generic design); Vítor Luís Rodrigues; António Martins-Tuválkin (2004; this specific v ... 16
Image Source: https://en.wikipedia.org/w/index.php?title=File:Flag_of_Romania.svg Contributors: AdiJapan ... 16
Image Source: https://en.wikipedia.org/w/index.php?title=File:Flag_of_Russia.svg License: Public Domain Contributors: Anomie, Jo-Jo Eumerus, Zscout370 ... 16
Image Source: https://en.wikipedia.org/w/index.php?title=File:Flag_of_San_Marino.svg Contributors: Zscout370 ... 16
Image Source: https://en.wikipedia.org/w/index.php?title=File:Flag_of_Serbia.svg License: Public Domain Contributors: ABF, Ankry, Avala, B1mbo, Begoon, Carnervan, Cantons-de-l'Est, Cathy Richards, Creepfip, Cycn, Denelson83, EDUCA33E, Ebrahim, Erlenmeyer, Fry1989, Guanaco, Herbythyme, Homo lupus, Illegitimate Barrister, Imbris∼commonswiki, Maks Stirlitz, Mattes, Mormegil, Nightstallion, Nikola Smolenski, Nuno Gabriel Cabral∼commonswiki, Odder, OgreBot 2, PhilKnight, R-41∼commonswiki, Rainman∼commonswiki, Rodejong, Rokerismoravee, Sangjinhwa, Sarang, Sasa Stefanovic, SiBr4, Siebrand, TFCforever, ThomasPusch, Torsch, Túrelio, WhiteWriter, Zscout370, Абдулло-Довуд, Добромир Костадинов, Ранко Николиħ, 12 anonymous edits ... 16
Image Source: https://en.wikipedia.org/w/index.php?title=File:Flag_of_Slovakia.svg License: Public Domain Contributors: Achim1999, B1mbo, Cycn, Erlenmeyer, Fry1989, Herbythyme, Homo lupus, IP 84.5∼commonswiki, Illegitimate Barrister, J 1982, Justass, Klemen Kocjancic, Leyo, Madden, Mattes, Mogelzahn, Mxn, Nightstallion, Peter Zelizňák, Pmsyyz, Pumbaa80, Ricordisamoa, Ruwolf, SKopp, Samah10, Sangjinhwa, Sarang, SiBr4, Srtxg, Str4nd, TFCforever, Torsch, Tvdm, Wiki-vr, Zscout370, 11 anonymous edits ... 16
Image Source: https://en.wikipedia.org/w/index.php?title=File:Flag_of_Slovenia.svg License: Public Domain Contributors: User:Achim1999 .. 17
Image Source: https://en.wikipedia.org/w/index.php?title=File:Flag_of_Spain.svg License: Public Domain Contributors: Anomie, Jo-Jo Eumerus, Topbanana ... 17
Image Source: https://en.wikipedia.org/w/index.php?title=File:Flag_of_Sweden.svg License: Public Domain Contributors: Anomie, Jo-Jo Eumerus, Mr. Stradivarius ... 17
Image Source: https://en.wikipedia.org/w/index.php?title=File:Flag_of_Switzerland.svg License: Public Domain Contributors: User:Marc Mongenet Credits: User:-xfi- User:Zscout370 ... 17
Image Source: https://en.wikipedia.org/w/index.php?title=File:Flag_of_Ukraine.svg License: Public Domain Contributors: Ahonc, Akhristov, Albedo-ukr, Andrew J.Kurbiko, Antonanton∼commonswiki, Chase 1, Cycn, Denelson83, Diánmondin, Dzordzm, Fred J, GoldenRainbow, Homo lupus, Ilyaroz, IvanOS, Jdx, Jon Harald Søby, Justass, Klemen Kocjancic, Kwasura, LlsnykMaria, Mattes, Maximaximax, Mormegil, Neq00, Odder, PsichoP-uzo, Sangjinhwa, Sarang, SeNeKa∼commonswiki, Serhio∼commonswiki, SiBr4, Steinsplitter, TFerenczy, Tat1642, User000name, Yann, Zcout1993, ZooFari, Zscout370, Живот Олегович, МЕИ, Ранко Николиħ, قف المزاري, على, 夢蝶葬花, 15 anonymous edits ... 17
Image Source: https://en.wikipedia.org/w/index.php?title=File:Flag_of_the_United_Kingdom.svg License: Public Domain Contributors: Anomie, Good Olfactory, Jo-Jo Eumerus, MSGJ, Mifter ... 17
Figure 14 Source: https://en.wikipedia.org/w/index.php?title=File:Moschea_00497.JPG License: Public Domain Contributors: user:Lalupa ... 18
Figure 15 Source: https://en.wikipedia.org/w/index.php?title=File:East_London_Mosque_-_panoramio.jpg License: Creative Commons Attribution-Sharealike 3.0 Contributors: Oxyman, Rafic.Mufid ... 18
Image Source: https://en.wikipedia.org/w/index.php?title=File:No-mosque.svg License: Creative Commons Attribution-Sharealike 3.0,2.5,2.0,1.0 Contributors: Albert Mestre ... 19
Figure 16 Source: https://en.wikipedia.org/w/index.php?title=File:Castillia.jpg License: Public Domain Contributors: Jdx, Liuscomaes, OgreBot 2, Paypayvay, 1 anonymous edits ... 22
Figure 17 Source: https://en.wikipedia.org/w/index.php?title=File:Great_Mosque_of_Kairouan_Panorama_-_Grande_Mosquée_de_Kairouan_Panorama.jpg License: Creative Commons Attribution-Sharealike 2.0 Contributors: MAREK SZAREJKO from CLONMEL, IRELAND - POLAND 25
Figure 18 Source: https://en.wikipedia.org/w/index.php?title=File:Moorish_ceiling_at_the_Sala_de_los_Reyes,_Alhambra.jpg Contributors: User:BrugesFR ... 26
Figure 19 Source: https://en.wikipedia.org/w/index.php?title=File:MoorishIberia.jpg Contributors: Alfonso X (Life time: 1221-1284) ... 26
Figure 20 Source: https://en.wikipedia.org/w/index.php?title=File:Cantigas_battle.jpg License: Public Domain Contributors: Acoma, Eurodyne, HaEr48, 1 anonymous edits ... 28
Figure 21 Source: https://en.wikipedia.org/w/index.php?title=File:Warriors_embrace_CSM_185_panel_2.jpg Contributors: Alfonso X (Life time: 1221-1284) ... 29
Figure 22 Source: https://en.wikipedia.org/w/index.php?title=File:Alhambra_Dec_2004_5.jpg License: GNU Free Documentation License Contributors: Anual, Balbo, Discanto, JMCC1, Javier Carro, Jbribeiro1, Joseulgon, Konstantin∼commonswiki, MGA73bot2, Mircea, 1 anonymous edits ... 30
Figure 23 Source: https://en.wikipedia.org/w/index.php?title=File:MuslimMusiciansAtTheCourtOfRoger.JPG License: Public Domain Contributors: Bohème, BotMultichill, DenghiúComm, Fleur-de-farine, Jbribeiro1, Memorato, Mhmrodrigues, Tarook97, World Imaging, 1 anonymous edits ... 31
Figure 24 Source: https://en.wikipedia.org/w/index.php?title=File:Spain_Andalusia_Cordoba_BW_2015-10-27_13-54-14.jpg Contributors: user:Berthold Werner ... 32
Figure 25 Source: https://en.wikipedia.org/w/index.php?title=File:Escudo_d'Aragón.svg Contributors: AnonMoos, AnonX, BrightRaven, CHV, Darwln, DenghiúComm, Ecelan, Frombenny∼commonswiki, Heralder, Herrinsa, Jed, Jimmy44, Joanbanjo, JotaCartas, Latoma, Macondo, Willtron, Xavigivax, 6 anonymous edits ... 33
Figure 26 Source: https://en.wikipedia.org License: Creative Commons Zero Contributors: User:Lobsterthermidor ... 34
Figure 27 Source: https://en.wikipedia.org/w/index.php?title=File:Royal_Standard_of_Nasrid_Dynasty_Kingdom_of_Grenade.svg License: Creative Commons Attribution-Share Alike Contributors: SanchoPanzaXXI ... 34
Figure 28 Source: https://en.wikipedia.org/w/index.php?title=File:Moorishbarbarians.jpg License: Public Domain Contributors: 1739 ... 35
Figure 29 Source: https://en.wikipedia.org/w/index.php?title=File:AverroesColor.jpg License: Public Domain Contributors: Admrboltz, Chenspec, Chyah, Frank C. Müller, Jane023, Jcb, Mattes, Sailko, Sparkit, 1 anonymous edits ... 36
Image Source: https://en.wikipedia.org/w/index.php?title=File:Wiktionary-logo-en-v2.svg Contributors: User:Dan Polansky, User:Smurrayinchester 39
Image Source: https://en.wikipedia.org/w/index.php?title=File:Wikiquote-logo.svg License: Public Domain Contributors: Rei-artur ... 40
Image Source: https://en.wikipedia.org/w/index.php?title=File:Commons-logo.svg License: logo Contributors: Anomie, Callanecc, CambridgeBay-Weather, Jo-Jo Eumerus, RHaworth ... 40
Figure 30 Source: https://en.wikipedia.org/w/index.php?title=File:Califato_de_Córdoba_-_1000-en.svg License: Creative Commons Attribution-Sharealike 3.0 Contributors: John of Reading, Morningstar1814 ... 42
Figure 31 Source: https://en.wikipedia.org/w/index.php?title=File:Map_of_expansion_of_Caliphate.svg License: Public Domain Contributors: DieBuche ... 44
Figure 32 Source: https://en.wikipedia.org/w/index.php?title=File:Map_Iberian_Peninsula_750-en.svg License: Public Domain Contributors: User:Little Professor ... 45
Figure 33 Source: https://en.wikipedia.org/w/index.php?title=File:Mezquita-Catedral_de_Cordoba_01.JPG License: Public Domain Contributors: User:Ploync ... 46
Figure 34 Source: https://en.wikipedia.org/w/index.php?title=File:Abdul_al_Rahman_I.jpg License: Public Domain Contributors: Jbribeiro1, Omar2788 ... 47
Figure 35 Source: https://en.wikipedia.org/w/index.php?title=File:La_civilització_del_califat_de_Còrdova_en_temps_d'Abd-al-Rahman_III.jpg License: Public Domain Contributors: Aavitus, BotMultichill, Elhananha, Exroader, Geagea ... 49
Figure 36 Source: https://en.wikipedia.org/w/index.php?title=File:Al_Andalus_&_Christian_Kingdoms.png License: Creative Commons Zero Contributors: Apocheir, Kilom691, Rocaralonso, SpanishSnake, باسم ... 50
Figure 37 Source: https://en.wikipedia.org/w/index.php?title=File:Hisham_II_of_Córdoba_Dinar_94227.jpg License: GNU Free Documentation License Contributors: CNG ... 50
Figure 38 Source: https://en.wikipedia.org/w/index.php?title=File:Empire_almoravide.PNG License: Creative Commons Attribution-Sharealike 3.0 Contributors: User:Omar-Toons ... 51
Figure 39 Source: https://en.wikipedia.org/w/index.php?title=File:Almohad_Expansion.png License: Creative Commons Attribution-Sharealike 3.0 Contributors: User:Omar-toons ... 52
Figure 40 Source: https://en.wikipedia.org/w/index.php?title=File:El_rey_chico_de_Granada.jpg License: Public Domain Contributors: Aavitus, BrugesFR, CommonsDelinker, FordPrefect42 ... 53
Figure 41 Source: https://en.wikipedia.org/w/index.php?title=File:Salida_de_la_familia_de_Boabdil_de_la_Alhambra.jpg License: Public Domain Contributors: BotMultichill, Bukk, Cookie, JMCC1, Macucal, Tiberioclaudio99, 1 anonymous edits ... 55
Figure 42 Source: https://en.wikipedia.org/w/index.php?title=File:Geschichte_des_Kostüms_(1905)_(14784104832).jpg Contributors: Flickr-viewK 2, Fæ, JMCC1, Kürschner, Wolfmann ... 55
Figure 43 Source: https://en.wikipedia.org/w/index.php?title=File:ChristianAndMuslimPlayingChess-cropped2.jpg License: Public Domain Contributors: Grey Geezer, OgreBot 2 ... 56
Figure 44 Source: https://en.wikipedia.org/w/index.php?title=File:Andalus_cantor.JPG License: Public Domain Contributors: ? - ... 57
Figure 45 Source: https://en.wikipedia.org/w/index.php?title=File:Granada's_sunset.jpg License: Creative Commons Attribution-Sharealike 3.0 Contributors: User:Alemangui ... 58

Figure 46 *Source:* https://en.wikipedia.org/w/index.php?title=File:AverroesColor.jpg *License:* Public Domain *Contributors:* Admrboltz, Chenspec, Chyah, Frank C. Müller, Jane023, Jcb, Mattes, Sailko, Sparkit, 1 anonymous edits 60
Figure 47 *Source:* https://en.wikipedia.org/w/index.php?title=File:Located_in_central_Spain,_70_km_south_of_Madrid._It_is_the_capital_of_the_province_of_Toledo..jpg *License:* Creative Commons Attribution-Sharealike 3.0 *Contributors:* User:Daytonarolexboston 61
Image *Source:* https://en.wikipedia.org/w/index.php?title=File:Italy_1000_AD.svg *License:* GNU Free Documentation License *Contributors:* User:MapMaster 65
Image *Source:* https://en.wikipedia.org/w/index.php?title=File:Simple_Labarum.svg *License:* Public domain *Contributors:* Aethralis 65
Image *Source:* https://en.wikipedia.org/w/index.php?title=File:Coat_of_Arms_of_Roger_I_of_Sicily.svg *License:* Creative Commons Attribution-Sharealike 3.0,2.5,2.0,1.0 *Contributors:* User:Heralder, User:The White Lion 65
Image *Source:* https://en.wikipedia.org/w/index.php?title=File:Petra,_Al-Khazneh.jpg *License:* Creative Commons Attribution-Sharealike 3.0 *Contributors:* User:Faraheed 66
Figure 48 *Source:* https://en.wikipedia.org/w/index.php?title=File:Arabo-NormanArchitecture.JPG *License:* Public Domain *Contributors:* Alan Liefting, Avron, BotMultichill, DenghiùComm, Mattes, Memorato, World Imaging, Zhuyifei1999 68
Figure 49 *Source:* https://en.wikipedia.org/w/index.php?title=File:MuslimMusiciansAtTheCourtOfRoger.JPG *License:* Public Domain *Contributors:* Bohème, BotMultichill, DenghiùComm, Fleur-de-farine, Jbribeiro1, Memorato, Mhmrodrigues, Tarook97, World Imaging, 1 anonymous edits 69
Figure 50 *Source:* https://en.wikipedia.org/w/index.php?title=File:Aghlabid_quarter_dinar_-_Ibrahim_II.jpg *License:* Public Domain *Contributors:* DrFO.Jr.Tn 70
Figure 51 *Source:* https://en.wikipedia.org/w/index.php?title=File:RogerReceivingTheKeysOfPalermo.JPG *License:* Public Domain *Contributors:* Giuseppe Patania 71
Figure 52 *Source:* https://en.wikipedia.org/w/index.php?title=File:Arabischer_Maler_der_Palastkapelle_in_Palermo_002.jpg *License:* Public Domain *Contributors:* Calame, DenghiùComm, EDUCA33E, File Upload Bot (Eloquence), G.dallorto, Jbribeiro1, JuTa, Pierpao, RobertLechner, Samuele Piazza, 1 anonymous edits 73
Figure 53 *Source:* https://en.wikipedia.org/w/index.php?title=File:ChristianAndMuslimPlayingChess.JPG *License:* Public Domain *Contributors:* Dbachmann, Shakko, World Imaging, Ángel Luis Alfaro, 2 anonymous edits 77
Figure 54 *Source:* https://en.wikipedia.org/w/index.php?title=File:TabulaRogeriana_upside-down.jpg *License:* Public Domain *Contributors:* TabulaRogeriana.jpg: Al-Idrisi*derivative work: PHGCOM (talk) 77
Figure 55 *Source:* https://en.wikipedia.org/w/index.php?title=File:Arabic_aristotle.jpg *License:* Public Domain *Contributors:* Alarichall, Ashashyou, Chiswick Chap, GeorgHH, Ilse@∼commonswiki, JMCC1, Joostik, Laurascudder, Orijentolog, Shakko, Urban∼commonswiki, الدبوني, 1 anonymous edits 78
Figure 56 *Source:* https://en.wikipedia.org/w/index.php?title=File:AverroesColor.jpg *License:* Public Domain *Contributors:* Admrboltz, Chenspec, Chyah, Frank C. Müller, Jane023, Jcb, Mattes, Sailko, Sparkit, 1 anonymous edits 79
Figure 57 *Source:* https://en.wikipedia.org/w/index.php?title=File:AverroesAndPorphyry.JPG *License:* Public Domain *Contributors:* Monfredo de Monte Imperiali 80
Image *Source:* https://en.wikipedia.org/w/index.php?title=File:The_Algebra_of_Mohammed_ben_Musa_(Arabic).png *License:* Public Domain *Contributors:* Fredrick Rosen 81
Image *Source:* https://en.wikipedia.org/w/index.php?title=File:The_Algebra_of_Mohammed_ben_Musa_(English).png *License:* Public Domain *Contributors:* Fredrick Rosen 81
Figure 58 *Source:* https://en.wikipedia.org/w/index.php?title=File:ChirurgicalOperation15thCentury.JPG *License:* Public Domain *Contributors:* Ashashyou, BotMultichill, Marcus Cyron, Orijentolog, Santosga, Shakko, World Imaging 82
Figure 59 *Source:* https://en.wikipedia.org/w/index.php?title=File:Liebig_Company_Trading_Card_Ad_01.12.002_front.tif *License:* anonymous-EU *Contributors:* Drdoht, Emha, Mary Mark Ockerbloom 83
Figure 60 *Source:* https://en.wikipedia.org/w/index.php?title=File:Ms.Thott.290.2°_150v.jpg *License:* Public Domain *Contributors:* Michael Chidester, Williams1998 84
Figure 61 *Source:* https://en.wikipedia.org/w/index.php?title=File:Westerner_and_Arab_practicing_geometry_15th_century_manuscript.jpg *License:* Public Domain *Contributors:* Anonymous painter,15th century 84
Figure 62 *Source:* https://en.wikipedia.org/w/index.php?title=File:Astrolabe_quadrant_England_1388.jpg *License:* Creative Commons Attribution-Sharealike 3.0 *Contributors:* PHGCOM 85
Figure 63 *Source:* https://en.wikipedia.org/w/index.php?title=File:Al-RaziInGerardusCremonensis1250.JPG *License:* Public Domain *Contributors:* Gerardus Cremonensis 87
Figure 64 *Source:* https://en.wikipedia.org/w/index.php?title=File:Syria_made_medicinal_jars_circa_1300_excavated_in_Fenchurch_Street_London.jpg *License:* Creative Commons Attribution-Sharealike 3.0 *Contributors:* Uploadalt 87
Figure 65 *Source:* https://en.wikipedia.org/w/index.php?title=File:Médaillon_Saint-Ouen7.JPG *License:* Creative Commons Attribution-Sharealike 3.0 *Contributors:* User:Giogo 88
Figure 66 *Source:* https://en.wikipedia.org/w/index.php?title=File:Arabo-NormanArchitecture.JPG *License:* Public Domain *Contributors:* Alan Liefting, Avron, BotMultichill, DenghiùComm, Mattes, Memorato, World Imaging, Zhuyifei1999 89
Figure 67 *Source:* https://en.wikipedia.org/w/index.php?title=File:Gentile_da_Fabriano_015.jpg *License:* Public Domain *Contributors:* Aavindraa, Anneyh, Emijrp, File Upload Bot (Eloquence), Herzi Pinki, Jastrow, Leyo, Mac9, Missvain, Sailko, SunOfErat, Zhuyifei1999 90
Figure 68 *Source:* https://en.wikipedia.org/w/index.php?title=File:The_Somerset_House_Conference_19_August_1604.jpg *License:* Public Domain *Contributors:* Alonso de Mendoza, Blue Tulip, BotMultichill, Botaurus, Clpo13, Conscious, Docu, Elsbeere, Enrique Cordero, Fadesga, Grubel, HajjiBaba, Infrogmation, Judithcomm, LTB, Mabrndt, Madmedea, Mattes, Oxyman, PKM, PierreSelim, Postdlf, Responsible?, Schekinov Alexey Victorovich, Shakko, Tiberioclaudio99, Verica Atrebatum, 4 anonymous edits 91
Figure 69 *Source:* https://en.wikipedia.org/w/index.php?title=File:Christian_and_Muslim_playing_ouds_Catinas_de_Santa_Maria_by_king_Alfonso_X.jpg *License:* Public Domain *Contributors:* Alfonso X, "The Wise" (13th century) 92
Figure 70 *Source:* https://en.wikipedia.org/w/index.php?title=File:Syrian_or_Egyptian_pieces_of_glass_with_Arabic_inscriptions_excavated_in_London.jpg *License:* Creative Commons Attribution-Sharealike 3.0 *Contributors:* Uploadalt 93
Figure 71 *Source:* https://en.wikipedia.org/w/index.php?title=File:Early_1500_Andalusian_dish_with_pseudo_Arabic_script_around_the_edge_excavated_in_London.jpg *License:* Creative Commons Attribution-Sharealike 3.0 *Contributors:* Uploadalt 93
Figure 72 *Source:* https://en.wikipedia.org/w/index.php?title=File:Venitian_glass_circa_1330_with_enamel_decoration_derived_from_Islamic_technique_and_style.jpg *License:* Creative Commons Attribution-Sharealike 3.0 *Contributors:* PHGCOM 94
Figure 73 *Source:* https://en.wikipedia.org/w/index.php?title=File:Roger_II_tari_gold_coin_Palermo_with_Arabic_inscriptions.jpg *License:* Public Domain *Contributors:* PHGCOM 96
Figure 74 *Source:* https://en.wikipedia.org/w/index.php?title=File:Offa_king_of_Mercia_757_793_gold_dinar_copy_of_dinar_of_the_Abassid_Caliphate_774.jpg *License:* Public Domain *Contributors:* User:PHGCOM 97
Figure 75 *Source:* https://en.wikipedia.org/w/index.php?title=File:Crusader_coins_of_the_Kingdom_of_Jerusalem.jpg *License:* Creative Commons Attribution-Sharealike 3.0 *Contributors:* User:PHGCOM 97
Image *Source:* https://en.wikipedia.org/w/index.php?title=File:Escola_de_atenas_-_vaticano.jpg *License:* Public Domain *Contributors:* Rafael 99
Image *Source:* https://en.wikipedia.org/w/index.php?title=File:Averroes_closeup.jpg *License:* Public Domain *Contributors:* Bibi Saint-Pol, Bukk, Denniss, Frank C. Müller, FranksValli, Ilse@∼commonswiki, JMCC1, Mattes, Orijentolog, Sailko, Sparkit 99
Figure 76 *Source:* https://en.wikipedia.org/w/index.php?title=File:MoorishAmbassador_to_Elizabeth_I.jpg *License:* Public Domain *Contributors:* Chesdovi, D Ambulans∼commonswiki, DarwIn, Ecummenic, Esetok, FishInWater, FunkMonk, G.dallorto, Iustinus, Luciusmaximus, Maculosae tegmine lyncis, Madame Grinderche, Mattes, Motacilla, Omar-Toons, Paul Barlow, Shakko, Wolfmann, Иван Дулин, 5 anonymous edits 101
Figure 77 *Source:* https://en.wikipedia.org/w/index.php?title=File:Sebastiano_del_Piombo_Portrait_of_a_Humanist.jpg *License:* Public Domain *Contributors:* Aa77zz, Aavindraa, BotMultichill, Bukk, FunkMonk, Jimfbleak, Jochen Burghardt, Lotje, Mario1952, MaxxL, OgreBot 2, Omar-Toons, Sailko, Shakko, 1 anonymous edits 103
Figure 78 *Source:* https://en.wikipedia.org/w/index.php?title=File:Arabic_astronomical_manuscript_of_Nasir_al-Din_al-Tusi_annotated_by_Guillaume_Postel.jpg *License:* Public Domain *Contributors:* Guillaume Postel 16th century 105
Figure 79 *Source:* https//en.wikipedia.org *License:* Creative Commons Attribution-Sharealike 3.0 *Contributors:* Uploadalt 106
Image *Source:* https://en.wikipedia.org/w/index.php?title=File:Gentile_Bellini_Madonna_and_Child_Enthroned_late_15th_century.jpg *License:* Public Domain *Contributors:* BotMultichillT, Breskit, HajjiBaba, Ham II, Mattes, Royalbroil, Shakko, World Imaging, 2 anonymous edits 106
Image *Source:* https://en.wikipedia.org/w/index.php?title=File:Re_entrant_prayer_rug_Anatolia_late_15th_early_16th_century_reverse.jpg *License:* Public Domain *Contributors:* Anonymous artist 107
Figure 80 *Source:* https://en.wikipedia.org/w/index.php?title=File:Suleiman_in_Veronese_The_Wedding_at_Cana_1563.jpg *License:* Public Domain *Contributors:* Coyau, Missvain, Pieter Kuiper, Shakko, Uploadalt, 1 anonymous edits 108

License

Creative Commons Attribution-Share Alike 3.0
//creativecommons.org/licenses/by-sa/3.0/

Index

Abbas ibn Firnas, 37
Abbasid, 48
Abbasid Caliphate, 27, 49, 58, 95, 97
Abbasid Revolution, 27
Abdallah ibn Buluggin, 61
Abdallah ibn Muhammad, 48
Abd al-Rahman I, 27, 47, 48
Abd al-Rahman ibn Habib al-Fihri, 48
Abd-al-Rahman III, 48
Abd ar-Rahman I, 37
Abd-ar-Rahman III, 27, 49, 57, 59
Abd el-Ouahed ben Messaoud, 101, 107
Abdul Rahman Al Ghafiqi, 45
Abu al-Fida, 108
Abu al-Hakam al-Kirmani, 59
Abū al-Hasan ibn Alī al-Qalasādī, 38
Abu al-Qasim al-Zahrawi, 49, 82, 107
Abū al-Rayhān al-Bīrūnī, 85
Abu Bakr ibn al-Arabi, 38
Abu Hafs Umar al-Murtada, 22
Abū Ishāq Ibrāhīm al-Zarqālī, 37, 92
Abū Kāmil Shujā ibn Aslam, 82
Abulcasis, 43
Abu l-Hattar al Husam ibn Darar al-Kalbi, 47
Abū l-Khayr al-Ishbīlī, 43
Abul-Qasim Ali ibn al-Hasan al-Kalbi, 75
Abu Mashar, 86
Abu Rayhan Biruni, 107
Abu Uthman Ibn Fathun, 59
Abyssinian people, 23
Adelard of Bath, 76
Admirals, 101
Afonso III of Portugal, 28, 43
Afonso IV of Portugal, 52
Africa, 102
Africa (Roman province), 23
Age of Discovery, 30
Age of Exploration, 86
Aghlabid, 65, 67, 68
Aghlabids, 3, 31
Ahmad ibn Muhammad ibn Kathīr al-Farghānī, 82
Ahmad Y Hassan, 117
Akhbār majmūʿa, 63

Al-Andalus, 3, 21, 27, 34, 37, 38, 41, **41**, 64, 70, 76, 82, 113
Albania, 1, 2, 13
Albanian language, 102
Albanians, 15
Albanians in Montenegro, 16
Albanians in Serbia, 16
Albanians in the Republic of Macedonia, 16
Al-Battani, 85
Al-Bayan al-Mughrib, 38
Albertus Magnus, 79
Alchemy, 37, 82
Alchemy and chemistry in Islam, 81
Alchemy and chemistry in medieval Islam, 76, 107
Alcohol, 94
Aldebaran, 76, 85
Al-Dhahabi, 107
Alembic, 94
Alentejo, 23, 47
Alexander Ross (writer), 109
Al-Farabi, 82
Al-Farghani, 107
Al-Firuzabadi, 107
Alfonso I of Asturias, 47
Alfonso VIII of Castile, 28, 51
Alfonso VI of Castile, 51
Alfonso VI of León and Castile, 43
Alfonso X, 77, 92
Alfonso XI, 52
Algarve, 23, 28, 43, 52
Algebra, 81
Algeciras, 51, 52
Algeria, 22, 23
Algerian War of Independence, 11
Al-Ghazali, 80
Algiers, 101
Algorism, 81
Algorithm, 83
Al-Hakam II, 27, 57, 59
Alhama de Granada, 33
Alhambra, 26, 30, 32, 54, 58, 100
Al-Hariri of Basra, 107
Al-Hasan al-Kalbi, 69

Al-Hasan ibn Ali al-Kalbi, 75
Al-Hassan al-Wazzan al-Fasi, 103
Alhazen, 107
Al-Idrisi, 77
Ali ibn Abbas al-Majusi, 88
Ali ibn al-Athir, 32
Ali Qushji, 108
Al-Isfahani, 107
Aljafería, 33
Al-Jannabi, 108
Al-Jayyani, 85
Alkali, 83
Al-Khazini, 85
Al-Khwarizmi, 81, 108
Al-Kindi, 82
Almagest, 78, 81
Al-Majusi, 107
Al-Makin, 107
Al-Mansur, 95
Al-Mansur Ibn Abi Aamir, 41, 59
Almanzor, 28, 42
Al-Maqrizi, 108
Al-Masudi, 108
Al-Maydani, 107
Almohad, 51, 57
Almohad Caliphate, 28
Almohad dynasty, 41, 60
Almohads, 43, 57
Almoravid, 51
Almoravid dynasty, 41, 43, 51
Almoravides, 57
Almoravids, 51, 57
Al-Muizz ibn Badis, 69
Alpujarras, 29, 54
Al-Razi, 107
Al-Sufi, 107
Al-Suyuti, 108
Al-Tabari, 107
Al-Tasrif, 37, 88
Al-Utbi, 107
Al-Walid I, 42, 44
Al-Waqidi, 107
Al-Zahrawi, 37
Amalfi, 95
Amir al-muminin, 74
Anatolia, 102, 107
Ancient Greek language, 22
Ancient Libya, 23
Ancient Rome, 95
Ancient world maps, 77
Andalusia, 42, 43, 100
Andalusian Arabic, 27
Andalusian people, 93
Andalusians, 27
Andalusi Arabic, 55
Andrea Bonaiuto, 60

Andrea di Bonaiuto da Firenze, 36
Angelus Silesius, 10
Anglo-Moroccan alliance, 107
Anglo-Norman language, 33
Anno Domini, 22
Antioch, 76
Apulia, 72
Aquitaine, 3, 45
Arab Agricultural Revolution, 43, 49, 69, 76, 94
Arab-Berber, 27
Arabesque, 68
Arabesques, 59
Arabic, 29, 90
Arabic alphabet, 102
Arabic calligraphy, 68
Arabic grammar, 107
Arabic language, 28, 41, 43, 66, 73, 82, 105
Arabic language influence on the Spanish language, 27
Arabic literature, 37, 104
Arabic music, 91
Arabic numerals, 84, 85
Arabic poetry, 107
Arab music, 76
Arab-Norman culture, 68, 89
Arab raid against Rome, 3
Arabs, 21, 23, 25
Arab slave trade, 5, 27, 101, 104
Arab World, 5, 104
Aragon, 33, 42
Archidona, 47
Aristotelianism, 37, 78
Aristotelian physics, 86
Aristotle, 78, 79
Arles, 45
Arms, 33
Ars dictaminis, 80
Art, 86
Artephius, 37
Arthur Augustus Tilley, 119
Artichoke, 89
Articulation (architecture), 32
Arzachel, 43, 82
Asad ibn al-Furat, 67
Asia Minor, 104
Astrolabe, 37, 85, 92
Astrology, 59
Astronomical, 105
Astronomy, 59, 104
Astronomy in medieval Islam, 37, 105
Asturias, 27
Athens, 9, 78
Atlantis, 43
Aubergine, 89
Avempace, 59, 86

128

Avenzoar, 43
Averroes, 36, 37, 49, 60, 79, 80, 85, 99
Averroism, 36, 37, 60, 79, 80
Avicenna, 86, 87, 107
Avicennism, 79
Avignon, 45
Ayyub ibn Tamim, 72
Azawagh, 23
Azawagh Arabs, 23
Azerbaijan, 1, 2, 13
Azores Islands, 5

Babylonia as the center of Judaism, 60
Badajoz, 48
Baghdad, 49, 58, 69, 78
Balkans, 1, 102
Baltic region, 6
Bangladesh, 11
Banū Mūsā, 82
Barbary coast, 4, 104
Barbary pirate, 101, 104
Barbary pirates, 4, 101
Bar-Hebraeus, 107
Bari, 31
Basque Country (greater region), 27
Basque language, 24
Batanalhaut, 86
Battle of Alarcos, 52
Battle of Bagdoura, 46
Battle of Cerami, 72
Battle of Guadalete, 41, 44
Battle of Las Navas de Tolosa, 41, 52
Battle of Río Salado, 52
Battle of Sagrajas, 51
Battle of San Esteban de Gormaz (917), 28
Battle of Toulouse (721), 41, 45
Battle of Tours, 25, 41, 45
BBC, 63, 118
Béjaïa, 24
Beja (Portugal), 47
Bejtexhinj, 102
Belarus, 7
Bengali Muslims, 21
Berber language, 41
Berber people, 43–45
Berber Revolt, 25, 27, 46, 67
Berbers, 21, 22, 37, 55
Berke Khan, 6
Bernard Lewis, 98
Bibliothèque Nationale de France, 106
Bilad Ash-Sham, 46
Biographical dictionary, 107
Birkbeck, University of London, 14
Birth rate, 14
Black Death, 52
Black people, 27

Black Sea, 6
Blazon, 33
Bodleian Library, 105
Book burning, 59
Book of Fixed Stars, 107
Book of Games, 77
Book of Optics, 82
Bosnia and Herzegovina, 1, 2, 13
Bosniaks, 15
Bosniaks of Montenegro, 16
Bosniaks of Serbia, 16
Böszörmény, 5
Brahmagupta, 83
Brethren of Purity, 59
Bristol Channel, 101
British Museum, 96, 97
Buda, 8
Bureau of Democracy, Human Rights, and Labor, 17
Burgundio of Pisa, 79
Burgundy (region), 45
Burkina Faso, 52
Butera, Italy, 72
Byzantine, 70
Byzantine Empire, 1, 24, 31, 66, 69, 85, 102
Byzantine Greek, 65
Byzantine Sicily, 3
Byzantium, 96

Calabria, 69, 72
Calbalazet, 86
Caliph, 44
Caliphate, 56
Caliphate of Córdoba, 27, 37, 41, 42, 57
Caliph of Córdoba, 49
Cambridge University, 105
Cambridge University Press, 75
Cantabria, 45, 51
Cantigas de Santa Maria, 22, 26, 29
Canting arms, 33
Capetian House of Anjou, 74, 95
Carolingian Empire, 51
Carpet, 91
Carthage, 24, 67, 79
Castile (historical region), 42
Catalan language, 41
Category:Islamophobia, 19
Catholic Monarchs, 29, 54
Caucasus, 1
Central Europe, 7
Centre for Public Opinion Research, 19
Ceramic, 100
Cerdanya, 46
Ceuta, 22
Cf., 119
Chain pump, 95

129

Chalcedonian Christianity, 65
Charles Martel, 25, 45
Charles William Previté-Orton, 115
China, 89
Christendom, 21
Christian, 24
Christianity, 1, 25, 72
Christians, 42
CITEREFGlick1999, 114
CITEREFHourani2002, 111
CITEREFPew 2011, 15–17, 111
CITEREFPew 2016, 15
Civil war, 27
Classical Arabic, 21
Classical language, 80
Classical mechanics, 37, 86
Classics, 22
Claudio Sánchez-Albornoz y Menduiña, 63
Collège de France, 104
Commons:Category:Al-Andalus, 64
Commons:Category:Moors, 40
Comparative religion, 38
Constance of Sicily, 74
Constantine the African, 78
Constantinople, 49, 66, 70, 102
Copernican heliocentrism, 85
Copernicus, 104
Córdoba, Andalusia, 42, 44
Córdoba, Spain, 37, 41, 48, 70
Corpus Aristotelicum, 78
Corsica, 21, 33
Cosmography, 78
Council on Foreign Relations, 112
County of Barcelona, 42, 51
County of Sicily, 65, 66
Covadonga, 27
Crimean Khanate, 5, 7
Crops, 92, 94
Crown of Aragon, 54, 74
Crown of Castile, 28, 43, 54
Crusade of 1101, 91
Crusader kingdoms, 76
Crusades, 23, 33, 76, 97, 99
Crypto-Islam, 54
Cultural Muslim, 1
Cumania, 6
Cypriot Turks, 15

Đakovica, 102

Damascus, 48
Daniel Defoe, 106
Dante Alighieri, 80
Dante Alighieri, 96
Danubian principalities, 5
De Lacy OLeary, 99

Delegation, 107
Deneb, 86
De Proprietatibus Elementorum, 86
Descartes, 81
Desert island, 106
Desert of the Duero, 47
Devşirme, 10
Dhimmi, 4, 56, 57, 71
Dhimmis, 114
Diccionario de la lengua española, 23
Dictation (exercise), 80
Diffusion of innovations, 76
Digital object identifier, 98
DIN 31635, 41
Dinar, 97
Dinars, 43, 97
Disputed statement, 109
Distillation, 94
Divine Comedy, 96
Doug Saunders, 112
Douro River, 47
Dulzaina, 91
Dunash ben Labrat, 60

Early Islamic philosophy, 37, 79
Early modern period, 21, 99
East London Mosque, 18
Edessa, Mesopotamia, 78
Edward N. Zalta, 99
Edward Pococke, 105
Egypt, 56, 68, 91, 102, 114
Egyptians, 23
Elizabethan England, 107
Elizabeth I of England, 101, 109
Emir, 48
Emirate, 66
Emirate of Bari, 31
Emirate of Córdoba, 27, 41, 42
Emirate of Granada, 4, 34, 41–43, 52, 53, 55, 56
Emirate of Sicily, 3, **65**, 76
Emission theory (vision), 86
Enchanted Moura, 24
Encyclopedia of Islam, 119
Encyclopedia of the Brethren of Purity, 37, 108
Endnote anone, 24
Endonym, 23
England, 5, 85, 101, 104
English language, 105
English literature, 105
Enna, 67, 72
Entrepôt, 53
Epistles of the Brethren of Purity, 59
Equatorium, 37
Eric Kaufmann, 14
Es:José Ángel García de Cortázar, 114

Esparto, 95
Essence–energies distinction, 79
Estevanico, 38
Ethnic groups in the Philippines, 23
Ethnonym, 21
Euphemius (King of Sicily), 67
Europe, 1, 89
European migrant crisis, 13
European miracle, 100
European Monitoring Centre on Racism and Xenophobia, 19
European Russia, 6
European Union, 11
European values, 2

Évariste Lévi-Provençal, 92

Existence precedes essence, 80
Exonym, 21
Expansion of the Ottoman Empire, 99
Experiment, 37
Expulsion of the Moors (1609–1610), 4
Expulsion of the Moriscos, 22, 27, 54

Fall of Constantinople, 7, 100
Fall of Granada, 22, 54
Fatimid, 68
Fatimid Caliphate, 31, 49, 65
Fenchurch Street, 87
Ferdinand III of Castile, 100
Ferdinand II of Aragon, 53, 100
Ferdinand II of Aragón, 29
Ferdinand Magellan, 30
Fertility rate, 13
Fibonacci, 85
Fielding H. Garrison, 116
Fifth Siege of Gibraltar, 52
Fihrids, 48
Filipinos, 23
Financial Times, 112
First Barbary War, 104
First coins, 95
First Fitna, 24
First novel in English, 106
First period (11th century), 41
Fitna of al-Andalus, 50
Flight, 37
Florence, 96
Folger Shakespeare Library, 40
Forced conversions of Muslims in Spain, 54
Foreign Affairs, 14
Foreign Policy Research Institute, 14
France, 5, 104
Francia, 48
Franco Cardini, 114
Franco-Ottoman alliance, 104

Franks, 25, 32, 45
Fraxinet, 3
Frederick II, Holy Roman Emperor, 32, 33, 74
Freedom of religion, 4
Freising (district), 34
French denier, 97
French language, 23
Fruits, 89
Fulbert of Chartres, 85
Fulling, 95

Gabriel Bounin, 105
Galbalagrab, 86
Galicia (Spain), 42, 47
Galileo Galilei, 86
Gallipoli, 9
Gastarbeiter, 11
Genoa, 96
Gentile Bellini, 107
Gentile da Fabriano, 90
Geographic coordinate system, 64
Geography and cartography in medieval Islam, 108
Geography in medieval Islam, 37
Geometry, 84
George Maniakes, 31
George Peele, 107
Gerard of Cremona, 78, 87
Gerard of Cremone, 76
Gerolamo Cardano, 85
Gharb Al-Andalus, 28
Ghayat al-Hakim, 59
Gibraltar, 44, 52
Giotto, 90
Giralda, 33
Giustiniano Participazio, 67
Globe Theatre, 119
Goa, 24
Goan Catholics, 24
Goan Muslims, 24
Gold dinar, 70
Golden age of Jewish culture in Spain, 3
Golden Horde, 6
Granada, 3, 24, 29, 47, 100
Granada War, 41
Grand Vizier, 8
Great Horde, 7
Great Hungarian Plain, 102
Great Turkish War, 7
Gregory Choniades, 85
Grove Dictionary of Music and Musicians, 117
Guillaume de Lorris, 86
Guillaume Postel, 104, 105
Guitar, 91

Hackett Publishing Company, 119

Hadith, 96
Hagar (Bible), 108
Haggadah, 57
Hajj, 36
Halo (religious iconography), 90
Hang gliding, 37
Hans Köchler, 20
Hans Talhoffer, 84
Hasan al-Samsam, 71
Hassaniya Arabic, 23
Hayreddin Barbarossa, 108
Hayy ibn Yaqdhan, 37, 105
Hazzan, 57
Hebrew language, 79
Henri II of France, 106
Henry George Farmer, 98
Henry Stubbes, 101
Henry VI, Holy Roman Emperor, 32, 74
Heraldry, 33
Hermes Trismegistus, 59
High medieval period, 76
Hindu, 24
Hindu-Arabic numeral system, 85
Hisham ibn Abd al-Malik, 46
Hisham II, 27, 50, 59
Hispania, 25
Historia Animalium, 78
History of gunpowder, 76
History of Islam in southern Italy, 21, 76
History of optics, 86
History of paper, 76
History of the Jews in Spain, 56
History of the scientific method, 86
Hockney-Falco thesis, 86
Hohenstaufen, 74, 95
Holy Sepulchre, 97
Horseshoe arch, 59
House of Barcelona, 74
House of Hohenstaufen, 74
House of Wisdom, 78
Hunayn ibn Ishaq, 82, 107
Hungary, 7

Iberia, 41
Iberian Peninsula, 3, 21, 25, 38, 41, 55
Ibn Abi Usaibia, 107
Ibn al-Athir, 107
Ibn al-Baitar, 37, 107
Ibn al-Banna al-Marrakushi, 107
Ibn al-Haytham, 81
Ibn al-Jawzi, 107
Ibn al-Jazzar, 107
Ibn al-Nafis, 106, 107
Ibn al-Qūṭiyya, 37
Ibn al-Shatir, 85, 107
Ibn Arabi, 38, 96

Ibn Bajjah, 37, 59, 108
Ibn Bassal, 43
Ibn Battuta, 36, 38
Ibn Hajar al-Asqalani, 108
Ibn Hawqal, 69, 108
Ibn Hayyan, 108
Ibn Hazm, 27, 38
Ibn Idhari, 38
Ibn Jubair, 70
Ibn Khaldun, 37, 79, 108
Ibn Khallikan, 107
Ibn Khordadbeh, 108
Ibn Miskawayh, 108
Ibn Rushd, 49
Ibn Sina, 49
Ibn Taghribirdi, 108
Ibn Tufail, 37, 60, 105
Ibn Zuhr, 37, 107
Ifriqiya, 44, 65, 67, 68
Ignác Goldziher, 11
Ilfracombe, 101
Immigration from outside Europe since the 1980s, 1
India, 24, 89
Indian-Arabic numerals, 81
Indian literature, 107
Indonesia, 30
Inertia, 86
Infectious disease, 88
Influence of Arabic on other languages, 76, 83
In situ, 35
International Standard Book Number, 19, 62–64, 98
Inventions in medieval Islam, 4
Ireland, 5, 104
Isaac Newton, 81
Isabella I of Castile, 29, 43, 53, 100
Islam, 1, 24, 65
Islamic, 97, 107
Islamic architecture, 11, 32
Islamic art, 4, 76, 89, 94
Islamic astronomy, 76
Islamic calligraphy, 59, 89
Islamic contributions to Medieval Europe, 4, 99
Islamic dress, 1
Islamic economics in the world, 4, 37
Islamic eschatology, 96
Islamic fundamentalism, 17
Islamic geography, 86
Islamic Golden Age, 4, 49, 76, 80
Islamic mathematics, 76
Islamic medicine, 76, 82
Islamic philosophy, 104
Islamic pottery, 76
Islamic psychological thought, 79
Islamic science, 11, 76

Islamic terrorism, 1
Islamic world, 76, 99
Islamic world contributions to Medieval Europe, 76
Islam in Albania, 15
Islam in Andorra, 15
Islam in Austria, 15
Islam in Belarus, 15
Islam in Belgium, 15
Islam in Bosnia and Herzegovina, 15
Islam in Bulgaria, 15
Islam in Croatia, 15
Islam in Cyprus, 15
Islam in Denmark, 15
Islam in Estonia, 15
Islam in Europe, 1, 2
Islam in Finland, 15
Islam in France, 15
Islam in Germany, 15
Islam in Greece, 15
Islam in Hungary, 5, 15
Islam in Iceland, 15
Islam in Ireland, 15
Islam in Italy, 15
Islam in Kosovo, 16
Islam in Latvia, 16
Islam in Liechtenstein, 16
Islam in Lithuania, 16
Islam in Luxembourg, 16
Islam in Malta, 16
Islam in Moldova, 16
Islam in Montenegro, 16
Islam in Norway, 16
Islam in Poland, 16, 19
Islam in Portugal, 16
Islam in Romania, 16
Islam in Russia, 16
Islam in Serbia, 16
Islam in Slovakia, 16
Islam in Slovenia, 17
Islam in Spain, 17
Islam in Sweden, 17
Islam in Switzerland, 17
Islam in the Czech Republic, 15
Islam in the Netherlands, 16
Islam in the Philippines, 23, 30
Islam in the Republic of Macedonia, 16
Islam in the United Kingdom, 17
Islam in Ukraine, 17
Islamophobia, 2, 19
Ismail al-Mansur, 69
Ismail ibn Hammad al-Jawhari, 107
Ismailism, 31
Ismail I, Sultan of Granada, 59
Istanbul, 109
Italian language, 23

Italian literature, 96
Italian maritime republics, 76
Italy, 5, 33, 65, 104
Ivan the Terrible, 7

Jabir ibn Aflah, 43, 82
Jabir ibn Hayyan, 83
Jābir ibn Hayyān, 82
Jaén, Spain, 47
James I of Aragon, 3
Janet Abu-Lughod, 95
Jan Janszoon, 101
Jean Buridan, 86
Jean de Joinville, 81
Jerez, 47
Jesus, 90
Jewish Encyclopedia, 113, 115
Jews, 56
Jizya, 4, 10, 42, 56, 71
Johannes Kepler, 86
John Greaves, 108
John Nelson (convert), 100
John Ward (pirate), 101
John Wycliffe, 86
Joint Jewish and Islamic philosophies, 60
Joseph F. OCallaghan, 114
Journey to Mecca, 36
JSTOR, 98
Judah Halevi, 60
Jund, 46
Jund al-Urdunn, 114
Jund Dimashq, 114
Jund Filastin, 114
Jund Hims, 114
Jund Qinnasrin, 114
Justinian I, 66
Jyllands-Posten Muhammad cartoons controversy, 1

Kaffir (racial term), 23
Kairouan, 44
Kalbid, 69
Kalbids, 65
Kalsa, 70
Kazakhstan, 1, 2
Kent, 101
Kepler, 86
Khanate of Kazan, 7
Kharaj, 4, 71
Kingdom of Aragon, 28, 51
Kingdom of Asturias, 28, 45, 51
Kingdom of Castile, 4, 51
Kingdom of Galicia, 28, 51
Kingdom of Granada, 28
Kingdom of Jerusalem, 97
Kingdom of León, 28, 42, 51

Kingdom of Navarre, 28, 51
Kingdom of Portugal, 28, 51
Kingdom of Sicily, 66, 72
Kingdom of the Asturias, 47
Kings Mosque (Pristina), 12
Kitab al-Kimya, 82
Kitab al-Miraj, 96
Konkani language, 24
Koran, 11
Kosovo, 1, 2, 12, 13
Kosovo Albanians, 16
Kris, 30
Kufic, 90

La Convivencia, 3
Ladino language, 79
La Reconquista, 4
Latin, 23, 82, 105
Latin language, 43
Latin translations of the 12th century, 4, 76, 86, 104
Latitude, 92
Laudian Professor of Arabic, 105
Layla and Majnun, 106
Lemon, 69
Leo Africanus, 23, 38, 103
Leonardo Fibonacci, 76
León (province), 47
Levant, 56, 76
Lexicography, 107
Lex Mahumet pseudoprophete, 11
Liber Abaci, 85
Liebigs Extract of Meat Company, 83
Linguistics, 37
Lipka Tatar, 7
Lisbon, 23
List of Arabic loanwords in English, 83
List of Arabic star names, 76
List of Byzantine Emperors, 66
List of campaigns of Suleiman the Magnificent, 7
List of Chinese inventions, 76
List of countries spanning more than one continent, 2
List of inventions in the medieval Islamic world, 37, 76
List of Portuguese monarchs, 28
List of Rasulid sultans, 86
List of Umayyad Governors of Al-Andalus, 44
Literature, 86
Liutprand, King of the Lombards, 45
Logic, 59
Log pod Mangartom, 6
Log pod Mangartom Mosque, 6
Lombards, 45
Lombards of Sicily, 73

London Museum, 87, 93
Lower March, 48
Lucera, 32, 74
Ludovico Sforza, 24
Lundy, 101
Lute, 92

Maghreb, 21, 23, 38, 46, 51, 53, 101
Magnetic compass, 86
Maimonides, 57, 60, 80, 107
Mairu, 24
Majus, 56
Málaga, 47
Malay peninsula, 30
Mali, 23, 52
Maliki, 37, 38
Malta, 1, 21, 65, 72, 95
Maltese language, 73
Mamluk, 90, 91
Maqama, 107
Maranao people, 23
Marca Hispanica, 51
Marca Hispánica, 28
March (territory), 48
Margaret Smith (author), 116
Marinids, 52
Mark of Toledo, 88
Markward von Anweiler, 74
Marrakesh, 43
Marrano, 29
Maslama al-Majriti, 37
Maslamah Ibn Ahmad al-Majriti, 59
Mathematical notation, 38
Mathematics, 78
Mathematics in medieval Islam, 38, 105
Maure, 33
Mauretania, 22
Mauri people, 22
Mauritania, 23
Mawla, 44
Mayor of London, 119
Mazara del Vallo, 21, 67
Measles, 88
Mecca, 36
Medical school, 88
Medicinal jars, 87
Medicine, 59, 78
Medicine in medieval Islam, 37, 105
Medieval Europe, 76
Medieval technology, 92
Medina Azahara, 33, 49
Medina-Sidonia, 47
Mediterranean Basin, 42
Mediterranean Sea, 102
Mehmed III, 109
Mehmed the Conqueror, 12

134

Melilla, 22
Melkite, 78
Menke (star), 85
Mérida, Spain, 48
Mesopotamia, 56
Messina, 72
Michael II, 67
Michael Scot, 49
Michael Scotus, 78
Middle Ages, 21, 41, 56
Middle East, 78, 104
Middle-Eastern, 91
Miguel Asín Palacios, 96
Milan, 24
Mindanao, 23, 30
Mineo, 67
Mirror, 86
Moayyeduddin Urdi, 85
Momentum, 86
Monarchy, 65
Mongol invasion of Rus, 6
Mongol invasion of Volga Bulgaria, 6
Mongols, 6
Montenegro, 2, 13
Moorish, 92
Moorish architecture, 32
Moors, 1, 3, **21**, 40, 42, 66, 101, 107
Morgan Freeman, 36
Morisco, 4, 22, 24, 29, 54, 112
Morisco rebellions in Granada, 29
Moroccans, 23
Morocco, 14, 22, 23, 36, 76, 107
Moro people, 21, 23, 30
Mosaic, 89
Moscow, 13
Moses Maimonides, 79
Mosque–Cathedral of Córdoba, 32, 46
Mosque of Cristo de la Luz, 33
Mosque of Rome, 18
Mosque of Uqba, 25
Mozarab, 56
Mozarabes, 55
Mozarabic, 27
Mozarabic language, 55
Mudéjar, 112
Mudéjar revolt of 1264–66, 29
Muhammad, 44, 96
Muhammad al-Fazari, 83
Muhammad al-Idrisi, 37, 76
Muhammad ibn Jābir al-Harrānī al-Battānī, 83
Muhammad ibn Mūsā al-Khwārizmī, 82
Muḥammad ibn Mūsā al-Khwārizmī, 83
Muhammad ibn Zakarīya Rāzi, 83, 87
Muhammad I of Granada, 53, 58
Muhammad XII of Granada, 43, 54
Muhammed V, Sultan of Granada, 58

Muladi, 27, 55, 112
Muladies, 55
Muqaddimah, 37
Muqarnas, 59
Murad III, 109
Murcia, 47, 52
Musa ibn Nusayr, 44
Muscovy, 5
Musical instrument, 91
Muslim, 21, 23
Muslim Agricultural Revolution, 37, 105
Muslim conquest of Persia, 1, 6
Muslim conquest of Sicily, 3, 66
Muslim historians, 107
Muslim minority of Greece, 15
Muslims, 41
Muslim settlement of Lucera, 21
Muslims in Russia, 11
Muslims (nationality), 16
Muslim World, 38

Nabidh, 6
Naqareh, 91
Narbonne, 48
Nasir al-Din al-Tusi, 105, 108
Naṣīr al-Dīn al-Ṭūsī, 85
Nasrid dynasty, 34, 41, 53, 100
National Library of Medicine, 117
Natural philosophy, 105
Navarre, 42
Nestorianism, 78
Netherlands, 5, 14, 104
New World, 30
New York Public Library, 20
New York Times, 117
Niebla, Spain, 47
Niger, 23
Noria, 95
Norman-Arab-Byzantine culture, 66, 76
Norman conquest of southern Italy, 3, 72, 76
Norman people, 66
Normans, 31, 72
North Africa, 1, 25, 48, 56, 67
North America, 35, 104
North Carolina Law Review, 98
North Caucasus, 1
Northern Africa, 91
Northern Caucasus, 2
Noto, 66, 72
Nur Ed-Din Al Betrugi, 86

OCLC, 98
Odo the Great, 45
Offa of Mercia, 95, 97
Old Testament, 90
One Thousand and One Nights, 105

On the Soul, 78
Orange (fruit), 69
Orient, 94
Oriental carpets in Renaissance painting, 107
Orientalism, 11
Orosháza, 5
Otello, 36
Othello, 36, 107
Othello (character), 107
Otto II, Holy Roman Emperor, 69
Ottoman Empire, 1, 7, 8, 91, 99, 102, 108
Ottoman Greece, 9
Ottoman Sultan, 10
Ottoman wars in Europe, 7, 99
Oxford University, 105

Paintings, 91
Pakistan, 11
Palace, 33
Palermo, 65–69, 89, 96
Palestine (region), 78
Panchatantra, 107
Pantelleria, 67
Paolo Toscanelli, 86
Paolo Veronese, 108
Papal, 97
Paper, 95
Parachute, 37
Parasite, 37
Pargalı Ibrahim Pasha, 8
Paris, 79
Paris Mosque, 5
Passover, 57
PBS, 40
Peace of Buczacz, 7
People of the Book, 42
Pepin the Short, 48
Perfume, 95
Peripatetic school, 79
Persian language, 107
Persian literature, 102
Persian people, 81
Perspective (graphical), 86
Peter I of Aragon and Pamplona, 34
Peter IV of Aragon, 52
Peter of Castile, 52
Pew Forum, 11
Pew Research Center, 13, 111
Pharmacopoeia, 37
Philip II of Spain, 29, 30
Philip Jenkins, 14
Philippines, 23, 30
Philosophical novel, 37, 105
Philosophy, 78
Physics in medieval Islam, 37
Picatrix, 37

Pierre Belon, 104
Pistachio, 69
Platonism, 59
Podolia, 7
Pogrom, 74
Poland, 14, 19
Polish–Lithuanian Commonwealth, 7
Polish-Lithuanian Commonwealth, 5
Polish Tatar, 4
Polymath, 37
Pomaks, 9, 15
Pope Innocent III, 74
Pope Leo X, 104
Pope Sixtus IV, 54
Population Reference Bureau, 112
Populism, 2
Porcelain, 100
Porphyry (philosopher), 80
Port (nautical), 21
Portugal, 1, 5, 21, 42, 104
Portuguese Ceylon, 24
Portuguese Empire, 24
Portuguese language, 23, 24, 41
Portuguese people, 21, 23
Prayer rug, 107
Pristina, 12
Privateer, 38
Prizren, 102
Proscribed, 79
Protestant Reformation, 86
Provence, 45
Pseudo-Aristotle, 86
Pseudo-Geber, 116
Pseudo-Kufic, 90, 93
Ptolemaic model, 85
Ptolemy, 86
Pulp (paper), 95
Pump, 95
Pyrenees, 25, 27, 44
Pythagoras, 99

Qadi, 37, 71
Qanat, 69
Quadrans Vetus, 92
Quran, 88, 104, 106

Radical right (Europe), 2
Rageh Omaar, 63
Ramón Menéndez Pidal, 92
Raphael, 99
Rashidun army, 3
Rashidun Caliphate, 44, 66
Reaction (physics), 37
Rebab, 91
Rebec, 91
Rebellion of the Alpujarras (1499–1501), 54

Reception of Islam in Early Modern Europe, 99
Reconquista, 1, 3, 21, 23, 28, 41, 42, 53, 91, 99
Red Sea, 102
Reed (instrument), 91
Ref anone, 38
Religion, 15, 16, 86
Religion in San Marino, 16
Renaissance, 49, 86
Renaissance Europe, 99
Renaissance humanism, 80
Renaissance of the 12th century, 104
Republic of Macedonia, 2, 13
Rhazes, 82
Rhodes, 102
Rhombuses, 59
Rhône, 45
Richard A. Fletcher, 30
Richard Francis Burton, 11
Richard Hakluyt, 100
Rigel, 85
Robert Guiscard, 31, 72
Robert of Chester, 81
Robin Hood: Prince of Thieves, 36
Robinson Crusoe, 106
Rock crystal vase, 91
Roderic, 44
Roger Bacon, 86
Roger II, 72
Roger II of Sicily, 31, 73, 76, 77, 96
Roger I of Sicily, 66, 71, 72
Roman Africans, 23
Roman Catholic, 10
Romance languages, 23, 55
Roman de la Rose, 86
Roman Empire, 22, 23, 66, 100
Romanian language, 23
Romani people in the Republic of Macedonia, 16
Rome, 18
Ronda, 33, 54
Rosette (design), 90
Roxelane, 105
Rumelia, 8
Rus (people), 6
Russia, 1, 6, 13
Russian Empire, 9
Russo-Persian Wars, 6

Sacks of Córdoba (1009–13), 50
Safavid Persia, 99
Sagrajas, 41
Sahara, 52
Sahih al-Bukhari, 108
Said Al-Andalusi, 37, 59
Salé, 101
Salerno, 95
Samar al-Aṭṭār, 98
Samar Attar, 119
Sam Wanamaker, 119
Saracen, 23, 81
Sardinia, 21, 33
Scholar, 38
Scholasticism, 79
Science and technology in the Ottoman Empire, 107
Science in medieval Islam, 4, 104
Scientific revolution, 100
Sculpture, 89
Second period (12th century), 41
Secretum Secretorum, 107
Secularism, 36, 60, 79

Şehzade Mustafa, 105

Selim I, 102
Septimania, 21, 41, 42, 44, 48
Serbs, 102
Seville, 47
Sextant (astronomical), 92
Sharia, 4, 107
Shawm, 91
Shia Islam, 68
Sibt ibn al-Jawzi, 107
Sicilian Arabic, 65
Sicilian language, 66, 73
Sicily, 21, 66, 76, 95
Siculo-Arabic, 31
Siege of Narbonne (752–759), 48
Siege of Syracuse (827–828), 67
Siege of Syracuse (877–878), 68
Sierra Nevada (Spain), 53
Silk, 57, 95, 100
Silk Road, 76
Simon Kuper, 112
Simon Ockley, 106
Sin, 86
Skopje, 102
Slavery, 57, 104
Slavery in the Ottoman Empire, 5
Slovenia, 6
Smallpox, 88
Social sciences, 37
Society for Creative Anachronism, 35
Sociology in medieval Islam, 37, 108
Sofia, 8
Southern Italy, 69, 95
South Italy, 1
Spain, 1, 4, 5, 21, 76, 104
Spanish East Indies, 23
Spanish Inquisition, 4, 29
Spanish language, 23, 41

137

Spherical trigonometry, 81
Spinach, 89
Sri Lanka, 21, 24
Sri Lankan Moors, 21, 24
Stanford Encyclopedia of Philosophy, 99
Stanwood Cobb, 99
Stefan Uroš IV Dušan of Serbia, 102
St Mary Redcliffe, 34
Strabo, 22
Strait of Gibraltar, 25, 46
Subdivisions of Russia, 2
Suction, 95
Sufi, 59
Sufis, 102
Sugar, 95
Sugarcane, 69
Sugar cane, 95
Suleiman, 105
Suleiman the Magnificent, 108
Suleyman the Magnificent, 102, 108
Sultan, 8
Sunni Islam, 68, 102
Surgery, 37
Surgical operation, 82
Surya Siddhanta, 83
Sweden, 14
Switzerland, 3
Syracuse, Sicily, 31, 67
Syria, 102
Syriac language, 78

Tables of Toledo, 37
Tabula Rogeriana, 37, 76, 77
Tacitus, 22
Tafsir, 108
Taifa, 3, 28, 42, 50
Tangier, 27
Taormina, 68
Taqi al-Din Muhammad ibn Maruf, 107
Tarì, 95, 96
Tarifa, 52
Tariq ibn Ziyad, 25, 36
Tariq ibn-Ziyad, 44
Tatars, 6
Tatars in Romania, 16
Template:History of al-Andalus, 41
Template:History of the Arab League member states, 66
Template:Islamophobia, 19
Template talk:History of al-Andalus, 41
Template talk:History of the Arab League member states, 66
Template talk:Islamophobia, 19
Thabit ibn Qurra, 82
The Battle of Alcazar, 107
The Book of Healing, 88, 108

The Book of One Thousand and One Nights, 11
The Canon of Medicine, 86
The Compendious Book on Calculation by Completion and Balancing, 81, 108
The Eastern Origins of Western Civilisation, 98
The Economist, 112
The Globe and Mail, 112
The Guardian, 119
The Incoherence of the Incoherence, 37
Theme of Sicily, 65
The Merchant of Venice, 107
Theologus Autodidactus, 106
Theory of impetus, 86
The School of Athens, 99
The Wedding at Cana, 108
Third period (13th century), 41
Thomas Aquinas, 116
Thomas F. Glick, 62
Thomas Walker Arnold, 10
Thughur, 48
Timeline of Muslim scientists and engineers, 92
Titus Andronicus, 36, 107
Toledo School of Translators, 49
Toledo, Spain, 33, 43, 61, 76
Trade, 56
Traditional Berber religion, 25
Tragedy, 105
Transmission of the Greek Classics, 76, 78
Treaty of Granada (1491), 29
Treaty of Karlowitz, 7, 9
Tree of Wisdom, 59
Troubadour, 91
Tunis, 49
Tunisia, 23, 67, 68
Turban, 108
Turkey, 1, 2, 9, 13, 14
Turkic peoples, 7
Türkischer Tempel, 11
Turkish Abductions, 5, 104
Turkish language, 107
Turkish people, 11
Turks in Bulgaria, 15
Turks in Europe, 11
Turks in Romania, 16
Turks in the Republic of Macedonia, 16
Tusi-couple, 85, 104

Ukraine, 6
Umayyad, 37, 41, 44
Umayyad Caliphate, 24, 27, 42, 44
Umayyad conquest of Hispania, 3, 21, 36, 41, 42
Umayyad conquest of North Africa, 67
UNESCO, 64, 117
UNHCR, 111

Unitarianism, 101
United States, 104
University of Illinois, 117
University of Naples, 116
Unsupported attributions, 100
Upper March, 48
Uqba ibn Nafi, 25, 48
Uthman Ibn Affan, 66
Uthman ibn Naissa, 45
Utopian, 109
Uzbeg Khan, 6

Valencia, 54
Valencia, Spain, 51
Vandals, 43
Vassal state, 4
Vegetables, 89
Venetian glass, 94
Vexillology, 33
Victoria and Albert Museum, 40
Vienna, 9, 11
Vikings, 72
Violin, 91
Virgin Mary, 90, 107
Visigothic Kingdom, 44
Visigoths, 25, 36, 44
Vitreous enamel, 94
Vlachs, 102
Volga, 2
Volga trade route, 6
Vulgar Latin, 65

Water clock, 95
Western Europe, 36, 60, 79, 104
Western Sahara, 23
West Syrian Rite, 78
Wikipedia:Citation needed, 1, 9–11, 14, 31, 35, 58, 60, 100, 101, 109
Wikipedia:Link rot, 62
Wikt:alchemy, 76
Wikt:algebra, 76
Wikt:algorithm, 76
Wikt:camphor, 76
Wikt:Category:English terms derived from Arabic, 76
Wikt:chemistry, 76
Wikt:cotton, 76
Wiktionary:Moor, 39
Wiktionary:Moorish, 39
Wikt:moreno, 23
Wikt:sugar, 76
William II Canynges, 34
William II of Sicily, 71, 74
William IX, Duke of Aquitaine, 91
William of Auvergne, Bishop of Paris, 79
William Shakespeare, 107

William VIII of Aquitaine, 92
Wissenschaftszentrum Berlin für Sozialforschung, 17
World War I, 6

Yahya al-Laithi, 37
Yaqub, Almohad Caliph, 51
Yusuf al-Kalbi, 69
Yusuf I, 58
Yusuf ibn Abd al-Rahman al-Fihri, 48
Yusuf ibn Tashfin, 51
Yusuf II, Almohad Caliph, 52

Zakaat, 4, 71
Zaragoza, 33, 48, 51
Zij, 37, 85
Zirid, 69, 72
Zirid dynasty, 72
Ziyadat Allah I of Aghlabids, 67
Zurna, 91

www.ingramcontent.com/pod-product-compliance
Lightning Source LLC
Chambersburg PA
CBHW051344040426
42453CB00007B/410